Tequila Cocktails

TEQUILA COCKTAILS

75 CLASSIC AND CREATIVE AGAVE-BASED RECIPES

BENTLEY HALE

ROCKRIDGE
PRESS

For general information on our other products and services or to obtain technical support, please contact our Customer Care Department within the United States at (866) 744-2665, or outside the United States at (510) 253-0500.

Rockridge Press publishes its books in a variety of electronic and print formats. Some content that appears in print may not be available in electronic books, and vice versa.

TRADEMARKS: Rockridge Press and the Rockridge Press logo are trademarks or registered trademarks of Callisto Media Inc. and/or its affiliates, in the United States and other countries, and may not be used without written permission. All other trademarks are the property of their respective owners. Rockridge Press is not associated with any product or vendor mentioned in this book.

Interior and Cover Designer: Karmen Lizzul
Art Producer: Samantha Ulban
Editor: Cecily McAndrews
Production Editor: Matthew Burnett
Production Manager: Holly Haydash

Photography © StockFood / Leatart, Brian, cover and 120; © Biz Jones, pp. ii, 18; StockFood / PhotoCuisine, p. vi; StockFood / Janssen, Valerie, pp. x, 26; StockFood / van Tonder, Hein, p. 17; © Iain Bagwell, pp. 52, 69; StockFood / Gräfe & Unzer Verlag / Liebenstein, Jana, p. 70; StockFood / für ZS Verlag / Eising Studio, p. 88; StockFood / Harrison, Michael S., p. 104.

Cover recipe: Traditional Margarita, page 28

Paperback ISBN: 978-1-63807-890-6
eBook ISBN: 978-1-63878-291-9
R0

*To my friends, family, and coworkers who have continually
supported my obsession with foam and flower cocktail
experimentations throughout all these years. Thank you for
being the best taste testers a girl could ask for.*

Grilled Peach Sangria, page 72

Contents

Introduction

I've been slinging margaritas since before I could legally drink them. I was in high school when I landed my first serving job at a mom-and-pop Mexican restaurant in a small town just outside Los Angeles. As soon as I turned 21, I was promoted to bartender and learned how to make their signature secret margarita mix. From there, I was quickly thrown into the dreaded margarita Monday bar shifts, where I got to get up close and personal with tequila.

As I ventured into my early drinking years, ready to order cocktails at bars, I was already over the traditional margarita—I'd been there, done that, and made them at least a thousand times over. I learned early on that tequila was my favorite spirit (I had adverse reactions to vodka and wasn't a fan of whiskey), but I was surprised to see a lack of tequila-based cocktails on bar menus. I ended up having to modify my drink orders, swapping tequila for the main spirit in most cocktails. It's no surprise that I received many side-eyes and raised brows from bartenders, followed by the typical suggestion of trying a Paloma or tequila sunrise instead. Thankfully, in recent years, tequila and mezcal have started making their way onto more craft cocktail menus, so ordering drinks has become much easier. I've also enjoyed creating tequila and mezcal cocktails for different bars I've worked at and was thrilled to create more for this book.

Throughout my career in the food and beverage industry, I aimed to learn as much as I could about wine, beer, and spirits. I quickly began to discover how special tequila and mezcal are; they are filled with history, culture, and pride spanning generations of families and hard-working laborers. The agave plant, which tequila and mezcal are made from, for example, takes anywhere from 7 to 12 years to cultivate. If that's not dedication, I don't know what is.

My hope is that this book will get you just as excited about tequila and mezcal as I was when I first started researching them. In addition to teaching you all about these agave-based spirits, I'll show you how mixing cocktails can be easy, creative, and fun. This book is filled with 75 recipes featuring amazing classics, tasty modern takes, and brand-new creations that highlight how versatile tequila and mezcal can be. Before jumping into recipes, I'll help simplify home bartending basics, starting with an introduction to mixology and covering bar tools and techniques. I'll also break down the different types of tequila and mezcal. Hopefully by the end, you'll realize that tequila and mezcal shouldn't be used just for throwing back shots or mixing margaritas. They can stand up to any vodka, gin, or whiskey cocktail—and they might even taste better, too!

Watermelon Margarita, page 38

CHAPTER ONE

All About Tequila

Before we dive into recipes, let's explore tequila and mezcal in more detail by tackling the most obvious question: What is the difference? Tequila is actually a type of mezcal, but not all mezcals are tequila. Wait, what? Basically, the word *mezcal* has dual meanings. Primarily, it refers to the umbrella classification of a spirit distilled from the agave plant, which includes mezcal itself, tequila, and other lesser-known agave-based spirits. So tequila is a special type of mezcal that has its own set of rules and regulations—it must be made from the blue Weber agave species and must be produced in the region of Jalisco, Mexico, whereas other mezcals are mostly produced in Oaxaca, Mexico. The primary flavor difference between the two is that mezcal tastes smokier than tequila because it is roasted and smoked underground during production, while tequila is steamed in aboveground pots.

WHAT IS TEQUILA?

First, let's talk about the different styles of tequila, mezcal, and some other lesser-known agave spirits by digging into their flavor profiles, production processes, and histories and the ways to drink them.

Types of Tequila

It's important to understand the different classifications and styles of tequila when deciding which one to use in a cocktail.

There are two main categories of tequila: tequila mixto (mixed) and 100 percent blue agave tequila.

Tequila mixto has a minimum of 51 percent blue agave, with the remaining percentage coming from other sugars and additives. Typically, tequila mixto brands will be called "tequila gold" and are cheaper than 100 percent blue agave tequila. They are commonly used as "well" or "bottom shelf" brands in most restaurants.

There are four distinct types of 100 percent blue agave tequila.

Tequila blanco (also referred to as silver, crystal, or platinum) is the spirit in its purest form. It's not aged in any type of oak and rests in steel tanks for one to two months or is bottled straight after finishing the distillation process. Since there isn't any flavor influence from oak aging, tequila blanco is considered to be the strongest or harshest style of tequila. Tequila blanco is a better choice for mixing in cocktails versus sipping straight or on the rocks.

Tequila reposado is aged for 2 to 11 months in oak barrels. *Reposado* means "rested" in Spanish. The type of oak and how long the spirit is aged affect the final flavor profile of the finished tequila and are determined by each tequila producer. Tequila reposado becomes tinted with a light golden hue and takes on caramel, spice, and toast characteristics, which are inherited from the oak-barrel aging. This type of tequila is a good option for both mixing in cocktails and sipping straight or on the rocks.

Tequila añejo is aged longer than reposado, for at least one year. The longer aging process in oak barrels darkens the tequila to an amber color and makes for a smoother, more mellow tequila. Tequila extra añejo is aged for more than three years, making for an exceptionally smooth, complex tequila. Both the añejo and extra añejo styles are best sipped neat or on the rocks instead of being mixed into cocktails.

Mezcal and Other Agave Spirits

Mezcal is the second most popular agave-based spirit and has fewer regulations than tequila does. It is produced in different regions than tequila (primarily in Oaxaca, Mexico) and can be made from a variety of different agave species, whereas tequila can only be made from blue Weber agave. The mezcal production process has remained similar to its traditional origins: The heart of the agave plant (the piña) gets baked and roasted underground, giving the spirit its distinct smoky flavor. Like tequila, mezcal is also categorized by different aging styles with its most pure, unaged version being called *joven*, which means "young," followed by reposado, añejo, and extra añejo styles like tequila. Mezcal is commonly enjoyed straight but is starting to be used in craft cocktails as well. If you're looking to create a smoky or savory cocktail, mezcal is a great option and is often compared to Scotch because of its peaty, smoky flavor characteristics.

Other lesser-known agave spirits are raicilla, bacanora, and sotol. Raicilla is similar to tequila—just with sweeter tropical flavors—and is only produced in Jalisco from wild agave species. It has only recently been imported to the United States and is gaining popularity with tequila aficionados. Bacanora is only produced in Sonora and is made from wild agave species in that region. Sotol has recently been removed from the agave-based spirit family because the plant sotol has been reclassified and is no longer considered an agave plant species. Even though sotol is technically no longer considered an agave spirit, it is still a great option to explore. It is only produced in Chihuahua and has a flavor profile that's similar to tequila, depending on how it is produced.

History

I could draft a whole book on the history of tequila and mezcal, but I will keep it short. Throughout Mexico, mezcal is known as the "elixir of the gods" and is the center of Mexican folklore and mythology. For centuries, the story has been based on the Aztec goddess Mayahuel, the goddess of fertility and love who brought happiness to her people. She was later also named the goddess of maguey, the agave plant, because the very first agave plant is said to have sprouted from her gravesite after her death. The legend goes that, upon her death, a lightning bolt struck the agave plant and split it open, releasing its sweet sap that was said to represent the goddess's blood. Cooking the sap from the agave plant created the first pulque, a milky liquid made by fermenting agave sap. It wasn't until the 1500s, after the Spanish conquest of Mexico, that Spaniards taught the Aztecs how to distill pulque, which led to the development of modern-day mezcal and tequila. In the 1600s, after the Spanish government opened a trade route between Manila and Mexico, a Spanish nobleman built the first large-scale distillery in what is now Tequila, Jalisco. The well-known Cuervo family opened their commercial tequila distillery in 1758, followed by Casa Herradura in 1870 and the Sauza family's distillery in 1873. Fast-forward to today, and there are more than 140 tequila distilleries in Jalisco alone, producing more than 1,000 different brands of tequila. The majority of mezcal is produced in Oaxaca, Mexico, which is home to more than 570 distilleries, with more in surrounding states. If you want to dive deeper into the history and culture of these spirits, check out the suggestions in the Resources section (page 122).

Neat or In a Cocktail

Tequila and mezcal can be enjoyed both straight and mixed in drinks, but the production styles of each help determine the best way to enjoy them. For instance, añejo or extra añejo tequilas, which are typically aged in old bourbon barrels, are better off served neat to fully appreciate the toasty vanilla notes that are created from barrel aging. Usually, the more expensive a bottle is, the more care and attention have been given to the production process, and so it should be enjoyed in its original state versus mixing with other ingredients.

TELL-QUILA ME THIS

In addition to the types of tequila and mezcal styles outlined in this book, a few key terms are important to know when discussing tequila and mezcal.

Agave azul translates to "blue agave" plant.

Copitas are little ceramic cups that are traditionally used for mezcal tastings.

CRT refers to the Tequila Regulatory Council, a nonprofit organization responsible for the regulation, verification, and quality certification of tequila.

Espadín is the most common type of agave plant, accounting for 90 percent of mezcal production.

Jalisco is the state in central Mexico where 80 percent of blue agave is harvested for tequila production.

Jimador is an artisan or farmer who harvests agave plants to produce tequila, mezcal, or sotol.

Maguey refers to any species of agave plants.

NOM number is a unique, government-regulated distillery number that is put on each bottle of tequila. It shows proof of quality and that the distillery is an authentic tequila producer following all standards set forth by the CRT.

Piña is the heart of the agave plant, which is used to make tequila and mezcal.

Pulque is a milky alcohol made from fermented agave sap. Since it is fermented and not distilled, it is not considered a mezcal but rather the grandfather of all mezcals, being made before distillation techniques were invented.

Worm salt (sal de gusano) is a popular pairing for mezcal tastings.

COCKTAIL TERMS

Dash is a rough measurement of a small amount, like a pinch.

Dirty means adding olive juice or olive brine.

Dry is when a drink has more bitterness and less sweetness.

Dry shake is when you shake the cocktail ingredients in a shaker without ice. This is usually done with cocktails that have egg whites. A dry shake helps emulsify the liquids to create a frothy or foamy texture.

Float is when you want to add a little bit of liquor, syrup, or juice to the top of a cocktail, creating a visible layer.

Infusing means imparting flavor into a liquid by soaking herbs, spices, or fruit in it for a length of time.

Muddle is when you mash ingredients with a metal or wooden rod to extract their flavors.

Neat refers to liquor served directly from the bottle into a glass; also referred to as "straight."

Nose refers to aromas or the way something smells.

On the rocks is a drink order served over ice.

Rim means coating the rim of a cocktail glass in sugar or salt.

Shaken is when you shake the ingredients of a cocktail to mix it, usually in a cocktail shaker tin.

Stirred is when the ingredients of a cocktail are stirred together. This method is used when you want to limit the amount of dilution from ice that you get when you shake a cocktail.

Up is the term for when a drink is chilled over ice, either shaken or stirred, and then served in a martini or coupe glass with the ice removed.

Reimagined Classics and New Twists

The recipes in this book will cover popular tequila cocktails like the margarita, Paloma, and tequila sunrise, along with reimagined tequila versions of well-known classics like the Negroni, Bloody Mary, and old-fashioned. It also features contemporary tequila classics like the Brave Bull, Batanga, and the Siesta, along with brand-new recipes featuring several types of mezcals, tequila infusions, and homemade syrups.

A BAR BUILT FOR TEQUILA

Setting up a home bar can be overwhelming when considering all the ingredients and tools it takes to make delicious cocktails at home. I'll break it down and focus on the essentials you'll need to appreciate tequila and mezcal cocktails, helping you make quality drinks in no time.

Tequila, Mezcal, and Other Agaves

There are thousands of tequila and mezcal brands on the market, which can make it difficult to decide which bottles to bring home. It's tempting to buy a bottle of each style from a specific producer, but that can be expensive. Luckily, when you're mixing cocktails with tequila or mezcal, you don't want to use the super high-end styles, since you'll be mixing and diluting them anyway. That helps narrow your selection right off the bat. If you decide to start collecting specialty tequilas or mezcals or realize you enjoy sipping them straight, then you'll need to do a ton of research on tasting notes and customer reviews for specific brands before spending a lot of money on a bottle.

For fruity and sour cocktails, you will want to stick with tequila blanco or mezcal joven, since they pair the best with juice and citrus flavors. They typically range anywhere from $25 to $35 for a decent-quality brand. For smoky, spicy, or savory cocktails, you will want to use a slightly aged reposado style of either tequila or mezcal, which can range between $30 and $40 per bottle. If you are only making cocktails for yourself or a few people, you can purchase smaller bottles, usually available in 375-mL size, in order to save money or sample different varieties.

Types of Tequila and Mezcal

Here is a quick breakdown of the different types of tequila and mezcal used in the recipes throughout this book. I outline the different flavor profiles of each one, along with how they differ and suggestions for alternatives you could swap them with. If you're trying to limit how many bottles you purchase, I would suggest starting with tequila blanco, tequila reposado, and a joven mezcal for mixing in cocktails. Save buying a bottle of añejo or extra añejo for when you're ready to sip tequila neat or are hosting a side-by-side tequila tasting. The most popular, widely available brands are featured in the following chart with the most affordable brands listed first, followed by a higher-end brand.

LIQUOR	FLAVOR PROFILE	RECOMMENDED BRANDS	BEST FOR	SWAP WITH
Tequila blanco	Earthy, light pepper, citrus	Espolòn Blanco Patrón Silver	Mixed drinks, infusions	Reposado or joven mezcal
Tequila reposado	Oaky, honey, floral, vanilla	Corralejo Reposado Herradura Reposado	Mixed drinks, coffee or vanilla infusions, sipping straight	Añejo or añejo blanco
Tequila añejo	Caramel, smoky, oaky, raisins, vanilla	Hornitos Añejo Casamigos Añejo	Sipping straight	Reposado
Mezcal (espadín, joven)	Earthy, smoky, herbaceous	Del Maguey Vida Bozal Mezcal Ensamble	Mixed drinks or sipping straight	Reposado or blanco
Mezcal reposado	Oaky, white pepper, caramel	Yuu Baal Reposado Espadín Xicaru Mezcal Reposado	Sipping	Tequila reposado or joven mezcal

Liqueurs, Aperitifs, and Vermouth

Using liqueurs, aperitifs, or vermouth in a cocktail helps create a well-rounded recipe. They add more flavor and depth that support the base spirit. Liqueurs are sweet and help balance tart flavors in citrus-based drinks or add decadent flavors to dessert cocktails. Aperitifs are bitter and are usually used to create refreshing, dry cocktails. Vermouths are fortified wines infused with herbs and fruit, and they come in dry and sweet varieties. Dry vermouth is typically used in classic martini recipes, while sweet vermouth is used in Manhattans and Negronis.

Aperitifs usually have bittersweet qualities to them. Campari and Aperol are two popular brands that are used in a variety of classic cocktail recipes.

Coffee liqueur tastes great in dessert martinis or in rocks drinks. Kahlúa is a popular coffee liqueur brand, with others like Mr. Black and Patrón XO Cafe gaining popularity.

Dessert liqueurs are sweet and have flavors like chocolate, hazelnut, or almond. Godiva chocolate liqueur, Disaronno amaretto (almond), and Frangelico (hazelnut) are all popular brands of dessert liqueurs.

Dry vermouth is also known as white vermouth and has a white wine base. It's made with aromatic herbs and produced in a crisp, refreshing style.

Floral liqueurs are gaining popularity, with elderflower being the most popular. St-Germain and St. Elder are two brands that I have seen used in bars.

Fruit and berry liqueurs are frequently used in classic cocktail recipes like flavored margaritas or bramble cocktails. Chambord (raspberry) and Giffard Crème de Mûre (blackberry) are two of the most well-known brands of berry liqueur.

Orange liqueur is most often paired with tequila in margaritas. Triple sec is the common base-level orange liqueur, with Cointreau and Grand Marnier being higher-end brand names.

Spicy liqueurs are liqueurs made with different types of chili peppers. Ancho Reyes is a popular brand that makes two different styles: a smoky, red chili style and a green, crisp chili style. I call for Ancho Reyes liqueur in many of the spicy cocktail recipes.

Sweet vermouth is also known as red vermouth and has a red wine base. Each brand of sweet vermouth has a different recipe, but it usually includes herbs and fruit flavors and typically tastes similar to port wine.

Mixers, Syrups, Infusions, and Bitters

Mixers, syrups, infusions, and bitters are some of the most important parts of a cocktail recipe because they let you get creative with different flavor profiles. Using an infused tequila adds more depth to a cocktail than using the liquor on its own. But if a cocktail uses a very sugary juice or a thick puree, then the infusion flavors may be overpowered by the other ingredients. That's why it's important to pick your infusions carefully when adding them to a cocktail. You don't want to waste all of that time and money on your infusion if you aren't going to notice the flavors in the final cocktail. A good rule of thumb is to use infusions when making cocktails that have few ingredients in the recipe so you can really highlight the infusion's flavor.

Mixers and syrups complement the alcohol and liqueurs used in a cocktail and help round out and complete the recipe. Unless you're making a straight martini recipe, you will almost always use some sort of mixer or syrup in a cocktail. Bitters are small bottles of infused spirits or tinctures created to add complex flavors and aromatics to a cocktail. They can be shaken in a drink or added on top of foam to create cocktail art.

Following is a list of the mixers, syrups, infusions, and bitters used in this book.

MIXERS

▶ **Bloody Mary mix** is not only used for classic Bloody Marys, but it can also be added to savory cocktails or mixed with beer to create Micheladas or Bloody Beers.

▶ **Carrot juice** is used in the Carrot-Ginger Elixir (page 66) and is a fantastic way to add sweet and savory notes to a cocktail.

▶ **Citrus juices** (lemon, lime, orange, grapefruit) are used in a variety of different cocktails. They add tart or sour elements to a drink and are usually balanced out by using a syrup or liqueur. Fresh-squeezed citrus is always preferred over store-bought juice.

▶ **Citrus sour** (also called sweet and sour) is a blend of citrus juice, sugar, and water that is typically used in margaritas as well as other classic cocktails.

- **Club soda** is used in a variety of cocktails to add refreshing bubbles.
- **Cream of coconut** is typically part of a piña colada and is used in the Cabo Colada (page 42). It is a sweetened coconut syrup and is commonly confused with coconut cream, which is not the same product.
- **Escabeche brine** is spicy pickled jalapeño and carrot brine used in the Escabeche Martini (page 56).
- **Fruit purees or nectars** like peach, pear, guava, and passion fruit are typically used in frozen blended drinks.
- **Ginger beer** is a nonalcoholic ginger soda with bold ginger flavor. It is different from ginger ale.
- **Olive brine** makes martinis "dirty" and is used in the Rated R Martini (page 55).
- **Pomegranate juice** is used to introduce bright colors and incorporate sweet/tart flavors into a drink. It is also the base for grenadine syrup.

SYRUPS

- **Agave-ginger syrup** is a diluted version of agave syrup that is infused with ginger water. It is used in the Jalisco Mule (page 97), La Diabla (page 90), and Carrot-Ginger Elixir (page 66).
- **Agave syrup** is a thick, sweet syrup made from the agave plant that is used in place of simple syrup in many of the recipes in this book. It is also called agave nectar.
- **Chamoy syrup** is used as a rim for various spicy cocktail recipes
- **Grenadine** is a pomegranate syrup used in the Tequila Sunrise (page 30), Golden Hour (page 31), Pom Pom (page 46), and Frosty Peach Margarita (page 34). It is also a classic bar staple used in many cocktail recipes.
- **IPA syrup** is a sweetened, condensed IPA beer syrup used to make the Hoppy Sour (page 100).
- **Lavender-honey syrup** is a syrup of diluted honey infused with lavender water. It is used in the Beekeeper (page 85) and the Bruja Blanca (page 80).
- **Simple syrup** is a mixture of sugar and water and is the base to many of the flavored syrups introduced in chapter 7 and used throughout these recipes.

INFUSIONS

Once you get comfortable infusing tequila, you may want to start experimenting with all sorts of flavor combinations. Here, I've listed the infusions used in this book and encourage you to try out other options as well. The infusion flavors I've picked are simple, quick, and delicious and make for a great base for cocktails. Recipes for the following infusions are outlined in more detail in chapter 7 (page 105).

► Strawberry Tequila

► Pineapple Tequila

► Coffee Tequila

► Hibiscus Tea Tequila

► Rose Petal Tequila

► Spicy Chile Pepper Tequila

BITTERS

Peychaud's or Angostura bitters are the most popular and widely used bitters in classic cocktail recipes. In recent years, a huge variety of unique bitter flavors have come on the market, and many bartenders and cocktail aficionados are making their own. In this book, we use the two classic aromatic bitters along with orange bitters, spicy bitters, black walnut bitters, and palo santo bitters.

Garnishes

Working with garnishes is one of my favorite things about making cocktails. They can range from something deliciously simple, like an aromatic expressed orange peel, to something beautiful, like an edible flower. Or they can be fun and unique, like a mini origami crane or a smoking rosemary sprig. Garnishes let you get creative with the cocktail, adding to the visual and aromatic elements of the drink.

► **Edible flowers:** These are some of my favorite garnishes to use because they add beautiful, eye-catching flare to drinks. Marigolds, peonies, and orchids are great options. Dried, tea-grade flower petals also work well and are easy to find online.

- **Fresh fruit:** Using a piece of fresh fruit that is featured in your drink is a classic, effortless way to highlight the ingredients in your cocktail.
- **Fresh herbs:** Mint, rosemary, sage, and thyme are all great herbs that are regularly featured in cocktail recipes. Mint tends to be used for refreshing summer cocktails, while rosemary and sage are more common in savory fall cocktails.
- **Olives:** These are a classic martini garnish. Stuffed gourmet olives add an elevated touch.
- **Specialty salt or sugar rims:** There are a variety of salt options to use instead of plain, white cocktail salt. You could try pink Himalayan salt, black lava salt, or Tajín seasoning or try making your own custom sugar or salt blends with dried flower petals.
- **Spices:** Baking spices like cinnamon, cloves, and star anise are great for garnishing fall- and winter-themed cocktails.
- **Vegetables:** Bell peppers, carrots, and chile peppers are some savory options to use in drinks like Bloody Marys or spicy margaritas.

Glassware

Picking the right glassware can make or break a cocktail. Not only do you want to make sure all the ingredients will fit in the proper glass, but you also want to present your cocktail in the best way possible. Martinis are always served in either a martini glass, coupe glass, or Nick & Nora glass. Rocks drinks can be served in pint glasses; short, old-fashioned glasses; wine glasses; or tall highball glasses. Margaritas come in a variety of different glass options, depending on style and preference. Here is a breakdown of some of the basic cocktail glasses that you'll need for your home bar. Feel free to shop for shiny, new glassware or explore local thrift shops for unique vintage finds.

- **Copper mule mug:** Copper mugs are traditionally used for mule cocktails, and some people believe that the copper enhances the flavor of the ingredients. At the very least, they definitely look cool and assist with keeping drinks ice-cold.

- ▸ **Coupe glass:** The coupe is a rounded martini glass originally used for serving champagne and more commonly used for craft cocktails. Smaller glasses are better suited for short-pour cocktails with fewer mixers, while the larger ones are good for recipes with more mixers.

- ▸ **Highball/collins glass:** Highball glasses are tall tumbler glasses used for rocks drinks with mixers or sodas. Typical highball cocktails would be a gin and tonic, Bloody Mary, Ranch Water, and Tom Collins.

- ▸ **Hurricane glass:** A tall, curvaceous glass often used to serve tropical mixed drinks like the piña colada and mai tai.

- ▸ **Martini glass:** This is a long-stemmed, V-shaped cocktail glass with straight edges. It is typically used for classic martinis, Manhattans, lemon drops, and cosmopolitans. These glasses come in a variety of sizes—smaller martini glasses are better suited for short-pour cocktails with fewer mixers, while the larger ones are good for higher-yield martinis with more mixers.

- ▸ **Nick & Nora glass:** This looks like a smaller-sized martini glass mixed with a coupe glass that has a long stem. It starts off in a V-shape but tapers into rounded edges. This style is typically used for short-pour cocktails with fewer mixers. I usually refer to them as the "cute" martini glasses.

- ▸ **Rocks/old-fashioned glass:** Rocks glasses are short, old-fashioned glasses typically used for drinks served on the rocks or neat. Some cocktails served in rocks glasses are the Negroni, whiskey sour, and White Russian.

Tequila Tools

Having your home bar stocked with the proper tools will help elevate your mixology game, but don't fret—you don't have to run out and buy a bunch of new items. You may already have some useful tools in your kitchen. If you're looking to purchase the basics, start off by investing in a cocktail jigger to accurately pour your ingredients and a Boston shaker set to get shaking and straining your drinks like a pro. There are a ton of affordable combo bar tool packs online that come with a shaker, strainer, bar spoon, and muddler for around $30. I would also suggest getting a citrus squeezer for juicing limes or lemons on the spot. Citrus squeezers are readily available in most grocery stores and kitchen supply stores.

- **Bar spoon:** This is about the same size as a teaspoon and is used for measuring out certain ingredients. Bar spoons also have long handles, making them perfect for stirring cocktails in a mixing glass.
- **Blender:** A blender is used for making frozen cocktails as well as purees, Bloody Mary mix, and some types of juice.
- **Boston Shaker:** A cocktail shaker set consisting of two glasses: a metal tin, typically 28 ounces, and a 16-ounce pint glass. You usually build the cocktail in the larger tin and cap the shaker with the pint glass to lock it in before shaking the cocktail.
- **Bottle opener:** Any bottle opener will do the trick—most can or wine bottle openers also have a beer opener on them.
- **Citrus squeezer/extractor:** This lets you make freshly squeezed citrus juice quickly.
- **Cocktail smoker gun:** A wide range of cocktail smoker gun brands are available to purchase online. Amazon has a ton of options that range anywhere from $30 to $100, but whichever brand you buy, make sure to get one with a hose attachment. You can also use a smoker gun on foods like cheese or fish, so it's a versatile kitchen tool to invest in and one of my personal favorite bar tools.
- **Corkscrew:** The waiter's corkscrew is my favorite type of wine opener because it also doubles as a beer bottle opener.
- **Cutting board:** You will need a cutting board for slicing various garnishes such as lime and orange wedges, lemon wheels, and cucumber slices.
- **Hawthorne strainer:** Use this mesh strainer for filtering out ice chunks, berry seeds, and pieces of fruit left behind from muddling.
- **Jigger:** This is an hourglass-shaped measuring cup with pour lines to make building cocktails quick.
- **Measuring spoons:** These are good for making batch cocktails or mixers like Bloody Mary mix, which usually calls for celery salt and black pepper.

- ▸ **Mixing glass:** You'll use this to mix cocktails before shaking or pouring into the final glass.
- ▸ **Muddler:** Muddlers come in either wood or steel versions. I prefer stainless steel muddlers with black corrugated ends that help break up the ingredients more than those with flat wooden or rounded ends.
- ▸ **Paring knife:** This small knife is best used for cutting small items like limes and lemons.
- ▸ **Rimmer tray:** This is a three-tiered salt and sugar tray for dipping your glass into a liquid first and then into a sugar or salt garnish.

ICE TO MEET YOU

Cocktail ice is the least expensive ingredient but the most essential addition to any cocktail. The type of ice you use in your cocktail has a significant impact on the final flavor of a drink. When shaking ice in a shaker tin, you'll want to make sure you have solid cubes that aren't too thin; otherwise they'll dissolve quickly and dilute all the flavors. Making large "mondo" ice cubes or round ice balls in silicone molds has become a popular trend with short-pour cocktails like old-fashioneds and Negronis as well as for serving with straight liquor pours. This style of ice cube should be made with distilled water to ensure you are making the cleanest ice possible. Crushed ice is also common in some cocktails like brambles, mint juleps, and slushy-style drinks. (If your fridge has an ice crusher, then you're set.) No matter what type of ice you're using in your cocktails, make sure that it tastes fresh and neutral. It's good practice to taste-test your ice to make sure it does not have any freezer funk or weird flavors in it before using it in your drinks.

Tagroni,
page 95

CHAPTER TWO

Mixing Drinks

Now that we've covered the basics, let's touch on technique and the practical aspects of making a cocktail. This chapter covers important methods and stylistic tips that you can use to get started on your own. I'll also give you pointers on throwing an exceptional cocktail party at home.

ESSENTIAL TECHNIQUES AND METHODS

The different techniques for making quality cocktails influence the texture and taste of the finished drink. You'll find these techniques mentioned in the instructions of most recipes, so make sure to pay close attention. Shaking a cocktail produces different results than stirring it, and forgetting to do a dry shake in a recipe can make the cocktail fall flat. Once you get comfortable with these techniques, you'll be well on your way to mixing cocktails like a pro.

Building in the glass: When you prepare the cocktail directly in the glass it will be served in.

Double straining: When you strain the drink in a Boston shaker through both a Hawthorne strainer as well as through a mesh strainer while pouring into the final serving glass.

Dry shaking: When you shake ingredients without ice to emulsify them in a shaker tin—this is usually done with cocktails calling for egg whites.

Muddling: When you mash the ingredients together with a muddling tool in a shaker tin before building the rest of the drink.

Rinsing/washing the glass: Typically done with vermouth or absinthe, when you pour a little bit of the spirit into a glass and roll it around to coat the inside before discarding the remainder. This allows for a hint of the spirit to be present in the final cocktail. This technique is usually used in dry martinis.

Rolling: A quick mixing of the ingredients by building them in a shaker tin and then pouring them out into another cup and then back in the tin to slowly combine them.

Shaking: When you shake to incorporate and chill all ingredients with ice in a cocktail shaker.

Smoking herbs: When you light an herb on fire and extinguish it quickly, allowing it to smoke. Serve the smoking herb as a garnish so it smokes during the initial presentation of the cocktail.

Spritz: A similar technique to rinsing the glass, this is done with a spritz bottle to lightly mist an ingredient, usually floral water or bitters. Spritzing can be done before the drink is poured into a glass or as a finishing touch over top of a drink right before serving.

Stirring: When you gently stir the ingredients in a mixing glass instead of shaking in a shaker tin.

IMPRESS WITH A FLOURISH

Flourishing is when you use certain techniques to incorporate a garnish into the final drink presentation. It's fun and takes a little bit of skill, but it can really elevate your cocktails to the next level by adding visual and aromatic flare.

Citrus twist or spiral: Adding a citrus twist not only brings a pop of color to a cocktail, but it also creates additional aromas that you get with each sip of the cocktail.

Clothespins: Using little clothespins to attach a garnish to the glass is a creative way to feature items that you don't want to float in your drink. I've seen origami garnishes or dried fruit peels pinned to a drink. I have even written little quotes on paper and used them as a garnish for a cocktail based on a famous author. This technique would be great for any themed cocktail party where you want to incorporate custom names or dates into a cocktail.

Create a sugar or salt rim: Dip the edge of the glass in either syrup or citrus juice and then dip it into sugar or salt so it sticks to the glass, creating a rim.

Flame a peel: This is when you twist and squeeze a citrus peel to release the volatile oils over a flame, causing the oils to quickly catch fire. It smells amazing and adds more aromatics to the drink.

Float herbs: Floating herbs add a rustic touch to the visual feel of the cocktail.

Rim a glass with citrus: This is when you take a citrus wedge or peel and rub it around the edge of the glass to lightly coat it, adding a subtle hint of citrus with every sip.

Smoking herbs: Adding a smoking herb, star anise pod, or cinnamon stick helps amp up the aromatics and creates visual appeal.

"Spank" herbs: Spanking herbs before placing them in your drink releases their essential oils, creating lovely aromas that you can smell with each sip.

PUTTING TOGETHER A COCKTAIL

How you build a cocktail is what decides the final outcome of your drink. There's a reason James Bond was so meticulous about his martini order—shaking or stirring a cocktail produces different results, as does the order of steps when building a cocktail. A tequila sunrise does not get its "sunrise" by adding the grenadine first, nor do margaritas get their salted rims unless they are dipped in salt first. Following recipes step-by-step will ensure you get a perfectly executed drink that tastes and looks the way it's supposed to. While it's hard to pinpoint universal cocktail rules because each recipe is different, there are some basic ones:

1. Try to use chilled martini glasses whenever possible.
2. Never shake bubbly drinks—always pour the bubbly ingredient in at the end.
3. Never over-shake or over-stir a cocktail because you will dilute it with the ice.

YOU'RE TEQUILA-'N IT: THROWING A COCKTAIL PARTY

Now that you've learned all about tequila, mezcal, and mixology basics, you're ready to host your first cocktail party—and I've got you covered! If there's one thing I'm really good at, it's planning a themed party. Here is a breakdown of all of the party tips and tricks you'll need to host a successful, fun, and stress-free tequila/mezcal event.

Setting Up

The three most important aspects of a party are the ambiance, the drinks, and the food. Setting up your space properly takes some time, but it is worth the effort to ensure you won't be running around worrying about tiny details—after all, you want to actually have time to socialize! Feel free to move your furniture around to create conversation areas and more space for gathering. It will help guests feel more comfortable and encourage everyone to mingle.

When setting up your bar, make sure to have a good cooler or ice bucket that will keep your ice cold. Display your liquor and mixer bottles with labels facing out and group bottles together by type. Display garnish options in one area for easy access, making sure to precut enough limes and lemons. Leave a sharp knife out with a small cutting board so people can cut their own citrus if you run out of precut garnishes. Make sure to have an ice scoop for ice and tongs for picking up garnishes. Set glassware out so your guests can grab a glass quickly without having to ask where you store them. It's also helpful to have a larger cooler filled with ice for chilling beer, wine, sodas, and water for guests to grab as needed.

If you're serving only tequila and mezcal, arrange them by type. When doing a tasting of different bottles, print out information about each bottle so guests can read about them and compare tasting notes. You could also take flash cards, fold them in half, and make little signs to place in front of each bottle. Make sure to include tasting information about each bottle inside the card as reference so you can compare your tasting notes with the producer's tasting notes.

When you are serving food at your party, it helps to keep things organized by having separate food and bar tables. If you're low on space, opt for setting your bar section up in your larger group space and keep food in the kitchen. People tend to gravitate toward the bar area, so you will want to have your bar section be the focus of the party.

Keep the Drinks Flowing

Having a margarita party? Try making a large batch of regular margaritas and offering additional flavor add-ins that your guests can use to build their own signature margarita. Set up a garnish bar with strawberries, blueberries, sliced jalapeños, and grilled pineapple. You can also offer different salted rim options, like black lava salt or Tajín seasoning. For mixers, you could offer several types of juices such as peach nectar, pineapple, or pomegranate juice. If you want to splurge a little bit, you could also offer a selection of flavored syrups or liqueurs for people to choose from, like elderflower liqueur, Jalapeño Simple Syrup (page 115), or top-shelf options like Grand Marnier or Chambord. Another cocktail sampler you could try would be a spread of different sangria recipes, like the ones on page 33 and 72.

For a DIY mixed drink setup, you will want to estimate about one bottle per every five or six people. One 750-mL bottle has about 25 ounces in it, which equates to around 10 cocktails per bottle. As with all cocktail parties, you will also want to ensure you have enough nonalcoholic beverages for people who aren't drinking along with water to ensure people are staying hydrated. Although you can't micromanage everyone's drinking habits, you definitely want to make sure you aren't promoting drunken debauchery.

Make It a Game

I am a sucker for games at parties. They are friendly conversation starters that help liven the mood. I personally love doing blind tastings where you hide the type of liquor and try to guess what it is just by tasting and smelling it. You could do this with assorted styles or brands of tequila. Another fun tequila-based drinking game is called the Standoff, where everyone stands in a circle with a shot glass. All the shot glasses are filled with water except for one, which is filled with tequila. Everyone has to take the shot that they are holding, and whoever gets the actual tequila shot has to answer an embarrassing question. You can also incorporate tequila or mezcal into your favorite party game. Get creative and have fun, but also be responsible.

A Round of Shots or a Tasting

Let's face it: When it comes to tequila, someone is always going to suggest taking shots. Shots can be a fun icebreaker, getting people to cheers and mingle with one another. Straight tequila shots are easier on the way down if you chill and shake them beforehand. Sliced lime wedges rolled in salt are a traditional pairing with tequila shots, as are orange slices dipped in worm salt for mezcal shots.

Want fancier shot options? Jell-O shots are always a fun party go-to. I have had lime Jell-O shots that were made inside a lime wedge and were super delicious. You can also use edible cucumber cups for your glasses in place of regular shot glasses—Cucumber Bombs (page 65) are sure to impress.

If you're planning to taste different tequilas or mezcals alongside each other, make sure to have a tasting bar set up with limes, oranges, and salt. You can get really fancy and have a spread of different salts like pink Himalayan salt, black lava salt, and floral salt (page 103). A proper tequila or mezcal tasting is best conducted when everyone has a specific glass for each liquor. That way you can compare and contrast while you're tasting them side by side. You can use basic shot glasses or mini plastic cups that are available at most grocery stores.

ABOUT THE RECIPES

Now that we've covered the basics, it's time to start creating delicious craft cocktails! Each recipe lists the tools, glassware, and garnishes you'll need and also includes tips or fun tidbits. A jigger will be used to measure all drinks, so we haven't listed this on every page. Tequila classics and new twists are spread throughout the chapters depending on the flavor profiles, making them easy to reference depending on what style of drink you're looking for, while the closing chapter outlines the homemade infusions, mixers, and syrups used throughout the book.

Tips

▶ **Make it a mocktail:** Many of the recipes can be made as mocktails, or nonalcoholic versions; just make sure to increase the juice or mixer counts if you are going this route.

▶ **Variation tip:** Many of the recipes have a variation tip, suggesting substitutions or different flavor options, especially if the recipe calls for a unique ingredient that may be hard to find.

Labels

Each recipe has a label underneath the title showing how it should be served:

▶ **Batched:** Premade, large quantities for serving punch-style or in pitchers (if not batched, each recipes makes one cocktail)

▶ **Hot:** Gently warmed, usually on the stovetop or with hot coffee

▶ **Rocks:** Over ice

▶ **Up:** No ice, in a martini-style glass

Cucumber Marjito,
page 32

Sweet and Fruity

Traditional Margarita

Rocks

Tools: rimmer, shaker, strainer, rocks glass

Lime wedge, for rim (optional)

Cocktail salt, for the rim (optional)

2 ounces tequila blanco

1 ounce orange liqueur (triple sec or Grand Marnier)

2 ounces freshly squeezed lime juice

1 ounce agave syrup

Ice, for shaking

Lime wheel, for garnish

The margarita: tequila's most well-known cocktail. There is no one correct way to make a classic margarita, and recipes can vary based on taste, but there are certain elements that should always exist in a margarita: tequila, an orange liqueur, sweet syrup, and fresh lime juice. In addition to variations on the margarita base, you also have the option of making them on the rocks or blended and, if you'd like, serving with a salt or plain rim. In this recipe, I've chosen a "skinny" version using fresh hand-squeezed citrus along with agave syrup instead of simple syrup.

▸ If you prefer a salt rim, rub a lime wedge along the rim of the glass. Dip the rim in the cocktail salt and set aside. Pour the tequila, orange liqueur, lime juice, and agave syrup into a shaker tin filled with ice and give a short shake. Pour the ingredients into a rocks glass and top with extra ice, if needed. Garnish with a lime wedge.

VARIATION TIP: Some classic margarita recipes call for a little bit of egg white to help round out the tartness of the lime juice and create a silky mouthfeel. It also creates a little bit of foam after straining. Use ½ egg white or a ½ teaspoon of egg white powder per margarita.

MARGARITA VARIATIONS

Blended or rocks: This is always a tough decision and usually depends on the weather.

Bulldog: A popular margarita trend uses small Corona beer bottles (Coronitas) that are placed upside down into the margarita glass so the beer slowly mixes with the margarita as you drink it. It looks super cool and is a great conversation starter. Quickly tip the beer bottle upside down into your glass, letting it rest against the side. This margarita variation is best served while sitting at a table instead of at gatherings where people will be walking around.

Cadillac margarita: A Cadillac margarita is a premium version of the standard margarita using a high-quality tequila reposado in place of tequila blanco and floating the orange liqueur, usually Grand Marnier, on top of the drink. Some restaurants will serve the Grand Marnier in a shot glass on the side.

Fruit: Strawberry, peach, mango, and coconut are all popular options when ordering margaritas at a restaurant.

Spicy: Muddle jalapeño slices and use Jalapeño Simple Syrup (page 115) instead of agave syrup. Use chili powder or Tajín for the rim instead of salt.

Tequila Sunrise

Rocks

Tools: highball glass

Ice, for serving

2 ounces tequila blanco

4 ounces orange juice

1/2 ounce Grenadine (page 117)

Orange slice, for garnish

Maraschino cherry, for garnish

The tequila sunrise dates back to the 1930s. This simple classic is a busy bartender's dream because it has just three ingredients—tequila, grenadine, and orange juice—and is poured straight into a glass. The reason it's served unmixed is to create the beautiful color variations that occur from pouring orange juice and grenadine together, making it look like a sunrise. Many people also call this a tequila sunset, but the recipe is the same. If you're anything like me, a sunset is an easier reference because I very rarely get the chance to catch a sunrise, especially after a few cocktails.

▸ In a highball glass filled with ice, pour in the tequila and orange juice. Slowly add the grenadine in a circular motion, allowing it to settle to the bottom. Garnish with an orange slice and a maraschino cherry. Serve with a straw and do not stir.

Golden Hour

Rocks

Tools: collins or rocks glass

Ice, for serving

2 ounces tequila blanco

2 ounces pineapple juice

1 ounce orange liqueur (triple sec or Grand Marnier)

1 ounce pomegranate juice

2 pineapple leaves, for garnish (optional)

Pineapple chunk, for garnish (optional)

Pomegranate arils, for garnish (optional)

This cocktail is an upgraded twist on the classic tequila sunrise and is referred to as Golden Hour or Magic Hour as a nod to the sunset lighting that photographers covet. In this recipe, the orange juice and grenadine used in the traditional tequila sunrise cocktail are swapped out with more sophisticated ingredients—pineapple juice and pomegranate juice, preferably fresh. The omission of super-sweet grenadine syrup makes this cocktail tarter and zingier, which is sure to make your lips pucker.

▸ Fill a collins glass with ice. Then pour the tequila, pineapple juice, and orange liqueur into the glass. Finish with a float of the pomegranate juice, slowly pouring it into the glass. The color of the pomegranate juice will trickle down the glass and blend in with the rest of the drink, making it look like a beautiful sunset. If desired, finish the drink off with the pineapple leaves, pineapple chunk, and pomegranate arils to get a perfect, hashtag-worthy cocktail photo.

VARIATION TIP: Many grocery stores carry an orange or pineapple juice blend that would work well in this recipe. Just make sure the juice blend you use is orange or yellow to maintain the sunset look in the glass.

Cucumber Marjito

Rocks, Batch, Serves 4

Tools: shaker, vegetable peeler, muddler, pitcher, rocks glasses

1 medium cucumber

12 mint sprigs, divided (8 roughly broken apart, 4 for garnish)

6 ounces tequila blanco

4 tablespoons agave syrup

8 tablespoons freshly squeezed lime juice

Ice, for serving

Club soda

4 lime wheels, for garnish

This is my take on a tequila version of a mojito, which is traditionally made with white rum. You'll be able to put your muddling skills to the test by muddling fresh cucumber and mint leaves with your favorite tequila blanco. Then you can work on your garnish game by making beautiful cucumber ribbons to decorate your glasses. This cocktail always pairs well with sweltering summer days, picnics, and barbecues.

▸ Cut the cucumber in half lengthwise. Cut half of the cucumber and place in a cocktail shaker. Peel the other half into ribbons by pulling a vegetable peeler lengthwise down the cucumber. Set the ribbons aside.

▸ Muddle the chopped cucumber, mint, and tequila in a shaker. Add the agave syrup and lime juice and shake to mix the ingredients. Pour the mixture into the pitcher with ice; then top it off with enough club soda to fill the pitcher, giving everything a quick stir to incorporate all the ingredients.

▸ Place your cucumber ribbons along the inside of each glass. Fill glasses halfway with ice; then add the muddled mixture to each glass. Garnish with a lime wheel and mint sprig.

VARIATION TIP: When muddling, add other fruit like blueberries, strawberries, or watermelon to give this cocktail more variety, or spice it up with a few jalapeño slices or a Tajín rim.

Amped-Up Sangria Roja

**Rocks, Batch,
Serves 4 to 6**

Tools: pitcher,
rocks glasses

1 bottle (750 mL) dry
red wine (Rioja or
Malbec)

½ cup tequila reposado

2 ounces agave syrup

1 cup orange juice

1 cup pineapple juice

1 orange, halved and cut
into ¼-inch slices

1 pear, cored and cut
into 1-inch pieces, plus
more for garnish

4 large strawberries,
sliced, plus more for
garnish

Ice, for serving

Sangria is a summertime staple from Spain. Classic sangria recipes vary but usually consist of wine, a sweetener, flavored liqueur, soda or another nonalcoholic mixer, and fruit. There are both red and white wine sangria variations that can be adjusted based on the season and what type of fruit is available. This is a tequila-loaded version of a classic red sangria—the spicy notes in tequila reposado blend wonderfully with red wine and fruit, providing an extra kick. Make sure to add pieces of the soaked fruit to each glass. I like to serve spoons with this drink to make it easier to eat the fruit at the end, but proceed with caution. I tend to drink sangria a little too quickly because I want to get to the drunken fruit pieces faster.

▶ In a pitcher, combine the red wine, tequila, agave syrup, orange juice, pineapple juice, and sliced fruit. Stir to combine and refrigerate for 2 hours or overnight. To serve, pour over ice. Make sure to include the fruit that has been soaking in the pitcher. Garnish with strawberry or pear slices and serve.

VARIATION TIP: The beauty of sangria is that you can use almost any type of fruit or wine to make a delicious and refreshing version of it. Get creative and try different combinations to find your favorite. You can change it up each season—try a white or rosé wine with peaches and berries for summer or add baking spices like cinnamon and vanilla to a red wine sangria during the holidays. Either way, you should end up with a tasty concoction.

Frosty Peach Margarita

**Blended, Batch,
Serves 4**

Tools: margarita
glasses, blender

**1 ounce Grenadine
(page 117)**

**1 (16-ounce) package
frozen sliced peaches**

8 ounces tequila blanco

**4 ounces orange liqueur
(Grand Marnier,
Cointreau, or
triple sec)**

**4 ounces freshly
squeezed lime juice**

2 ounces agave syrup

1 cup ice cubes

Mint sprigs, for garnish

**These delicious Frosty Peach Margaritas are exactly what
you'll want to have on hand when the sun is beating down.
The addition of grenadine makes these cocktails look like
beautiful Georgia peaches in the glass. Top them with a
mint sprig and fresh peach slices and they'll (almost) be too
pretty to drink.**

▸ Pour ½ ounce of grenadine into the bottom of each of the
margarita glasses and set aside. In a blender, combine the
frozen sliced peaches, tequila, orange liqueur, lime juice, agave
syrup, and ice cubes. Puree until smooth. Slowly pour into
the glasses over the grenadine, creating a beautiful orange
and pink swirl. Top each glass with a mint sprig and serve
immediately.

VARIATION TIP: Feel free to swap out the orange liqueur for
peach schnapps to give this cocktail an extra peachy kick.

Strawberry-Thyme Martini

Up

Tools: rimmer, martini glass, shaker, muddler, strainer

Sugar, for rim (optional)

3 ounces Strawberry Tequila (page 109)

1 ounce lemon juice

½ ounce Thyme Simple Syrup (page 114)

1 large strawberry, sliced

Ice, for shaking

Thyme sprig, for garnish

This is one of my all-time favorite martinis. Muddling fresh, ripe strawberries with strawberry-infused tequila is absolutely delicious. The Thyme Simple Syrup softens the tequila and pairs wonderfully with the strawberries, creating a fresh, herb-garden feel. The sugared rim allows for a touch of natural sweetness. If you love strawberries, this is the perfect martini that doesn't taste overly sweet and showcases fresh strawberries when they're in season.

▶ Rim a chilled martini glass with sugar (if using) and set aside. Pour the strawberry tequila, lemon juice, thyme simple syrup, and strawberry into a shaker; then muddle for several seconds. Fill the shaker tin with ice, and then shake vigorously. Strain with a Hawthorne strainer into the center of the glass, being careful not to mess up the sugar rim. Garnish with a thyme sprig.

TIP: This cocktail tastes best when using ripe strawberries. If the strawberries are not red all the way through and have white in the center, the drink may come out tasting too tart or fall flat.

Berry Bramble

Tools: shaker, muddler, strainer, old-fashioned glass

1 ounce freshly squeezed lemon juice

3 or 4 blackberries or blueberries, plus more for garnish

2 ounces tequila añejo

½ ounce simple syrup (page 114) or agave syrup

Ice, for shaking

Crushed ice, for serving

¾ ounce Crème de Mûre berry liqueur (or Chambord)

Lemon twist, for garnish

The bramble is an elegant, modern classic created in the '80s that has gin, lemon juice, Crème de Mûre (a blackberry liqueur), and crushed ice. This tequila take is just as refreshing as the traditional version and is best enjoyed when berries are in season. Crushed ice is hard to come by unless your fridge has an ice dispenser. If you don't have an ice crusher, a good old-fashioned smash job will do the trick (and could also help ease any tension or frustrations you might have). If you don't feel like hammering away at ice, then regular ice cubes will suffice. Crème de Mûre may be hard to find in most grocery stores but should be available in liquor stores. If not, Chambord (a raspberry liqueur) or another berry liqueur would work just as well.

▶ Muddle the lemon juice and berries in a shaker tin. Add the tequila, simple syrup, and ice to the shaker and shake until the drink is well chilled. Strain it into an old-fashioned glass over crushed ice. Gently pour the berry liqueur over the crushed ice in a circular motion. Garnish with fresh berries and a lemon twist.

VARIATION TIP: Make this a Royal Bramble by topping it off with a little bit of champagne for a sophisticated touch.

Nectar of the Gods

Rocks

Tools: shaker, strainer, rocks glass

2 ounces tequila blanco

1 ounce elderflower liqueur (St-Germain)

2 ounces guava nectar

1 ounce Citrus Sour Mix (page 106)

Ice, for shaking

Edible flower, or dried flowers, for garnish

Mexico is known for its popular juice drinks, ranging from agua fresca to a variety of nectar flavors, so it only makes sense to incorporate a nectar juice into a cocktail. Nectars work really well in rocks drinks because they are lighter in consistency than purees, which are usually used in blended drinks. Nectars can easily be shaken without changing the consistency of the final product. This recipe calls for guava nectar, but feel free to substitute your favorite nectar flavor.

► Combine the tequila, elderflower liquer, guava nectar, and citrus sour mix in a shaker tin filled with ice. Give the mixture a short shake to chill and incorporate ingredients. Strain into a glass and top with ice. Place an edible flower atop before serving.

VARIATION TIP: Don't have any Citrus Sour Mix prepped? Squeeze a wedge each of lime, orange, and lemon to make a quick mix on the fly.

Watermelon Margarita

Rocks

Tools: blender, shaker, strainer

1 small watermelon

Ice, for shaking

2 ounces tequila blanco

½ ounce orange liqueur (triple sec or Grand Marnier)

½ ounce agave syrup

1 ounce freshly squeezed lime juice

Lime wedge, for garnish

Kosher salt or Tajín, for rim (optional)

Every summer, one of my favorite Mexican restaurants serves its watermelon margaritas inside a mini watermelon. They run out of them quickly, so we make sure to make our dinner reservations early in order to get them. I love the presentation of the watermelon shell as the glass and the fact that you know they're using fresh watermelon juice from that same watermelon. If you're able to find small watermelons at your local grocery store, the extra effort in preparation is so worth the time for a great presentation. This delicious and fun cocktail will be sure to impress your guests.

TO PREP THE WATERMELON

▸ Slice off the top third of the watermelon and discard it. Score the remaining fruit with a knife along the edges of the rind. Using an ice-cream scoop or large spoon, scoop out the flesh and transfer it to a blender. Keep the watermelon rind shell to use for your serving cup. (You can cut a small piece off the bottom of the watermelon so it can sit flat on a surface or plate for serving, but make sure you don't cut through the rind.) Blend the watermelon until smooth, then strain it into a pitcher or bowl. You will have plenty of watermelon juice left over to use as you please—it will last for 1 to 2 days in the fridge.

TO MAKE THE MARGARITA

► Combine ice, the tequila, orange liqueur, agave syrup, lime juice, and 2 ounces of watermelon juice in a shaker and shake vigorously. Pour into your watermelon shell or a glass and top with ice, if needed. Garnish with a lime wedge if you like, and sprinkle the edges of the watermelon with salt or Tajín (if using).

VARIATION TIP: Add a few mint sprigs to the watermelon juice for a refreshing combination.

Batanga

Rocks

Tools: highball glass, rimmer, bar spoon

Cocktail salt, for rim

Ice, for serving

2 ounces tequila blanco

¾ ounce freshly squeezed lime juice

4 to 6 ounces cola

Lime wedge, for garnish

The batanga is a classic tequila cocktail consisting of tequila blanco, cola, lime juice, and salt. It's pretty similar to the popular Cuba libre but swaps the rum for tequila. The batanga was officially created in 1961 by Don Javier Delgado Corona, the owner of a popular cantina called La Capilla, located in a small town just outside Tequila, Mexico. The combination of lime juice and a little salt mixed with cola brings this simple cocktail to another level.

▸ Rim a highball glass with salt; then fill to the top with ice cubes. Pour in the tequila and lime juice and top with cola, stirring gently. Garnish with a lime wedge.

Brave Bull

Rocks

Tools: mixing glass, strainer, rocks glass

1½ ounces tequila reposado

1 ounce Kahlúa

Ice, for serving

Orange spiral, to garnish

A Brave Bull is basically a tequila version of the classic Black Russian cocktail, which is the dairy-free version of a White Russian. White Russians are usually consumed as an after-dinner drink and have three simple ingredients: Kahlúa, cream, and vodka. The Brave Bull features only two ingredients, which just happen to be Mexico's most popular spirits: tequila and Kahlúa. The name of this classic cocktail is said to have originated from the 1950s movie *The Brave Bulls*, which is a western-action movie about bullfighting in Mexico. This simple two-ingredient cocktail works well as a summer happy hour sipper or an after-dinner drink.

▸ Pour the tequila and Kahlúa into a mixing glass filled with ice and stir until well chilled. Strain into a rocks glass filled with large ice cubes. Garnish with an orange peel.

VARIATIONS: Swap the tequila reposado for coffee-infused tequila and use frozen coffee cubes instead of regular ice for a coffee-loaded kick.

Cabo Colada

Blended, Serves 2

Tools: blender, hurricane glasses

2 ounces pineapple juice

2 ounces Coco Lopez coconut cream

1½ ounces tequila reposado

1 ounce banana liqueur

½ cup diced pineapple, frozen

1 medium banana, peeled

1½ cups ice

Pineapple leaves, for garnish

2 pineapple slices, for garnish

2 maraschino cherries, for garnish

½ ounce spiced dark rum (Myer's or Kraken Rum; optional)

All it takes is one sip of a piña colada to be transported to a tropical island. This Cabo Colada is a take on the traditional piña colada, swapping out rum for tequila reposado and adding bananas—your first sip will have you thinking about vacationing in Cabo. Save yourself the heartburn and funky aftertaste by using homemade colada mix instead of store-bought. Once you make your own colada mix from scratch with coconut cream and pineapple, you'll never want to go back to using premade again.

► Combine the pineapple juice, coconut cream, tequila, banana liqueur, pineapple, banana, and ice in a blender and mix until smooth. Divide equally into hurricane glasses. Garnish with pineapple leaves, a pineapple slice, and a maraschino cherry. Float with spiced dark rum to add an extra kick (if using).

VARIATION TIP: If you can find edible purple orchids at your local grocery or specialty store, they are the perfect tropical drink garnish.

Zinger Club

Up

Tools: muddler, shaker, strainer, coupe or martini glass

6 raspberries, divided

2 ounces Hibiscus Tea Tequila (page 111)

½ ounce freshly squeezed lemon juice

1 egg white, or ½ teaspoon egg white powder

1 ounce agave syrup

Ice, for shaking

Hibiscus tea (*agua de Jamaica*) is one of the more popular agua fresca flavors consumed throughout Latin America. Many popular tea companies in the United States refer to their hibiscus tea blends as "zinger" tea, with the "zinger" name meaning that it has hibiscus in it. One of my favorites is raspberry zinger tea blend, so I immediately thought of one of my favorite classic raspberry cocktails—the Clover Club. The Zinger Club is a sophisticated tequila version of the Clover Club that highlights the hibiscus tea by infusing it with tequila blanco. Fresh muddled raspberries with a splash of fresh citrus shaken with egg whites make for an aromatic, tart, and velvety cocktail.

▸ Muddle three raspberries with the tequila in a shaker tin. Add the lemon juice, egg white, and agave syrup; then dry shake. Add ice and shake again until well chilled. Strain into a chilled coupe or martini glass. Garnish with three speared raspberries.

The Candy Shop

Rocks

Tools: saucer, rocks glass, shaker, strainer

1 (0.33-ounce) package Strawberry Pop Rocks, for rim

Tajín, for rim

Chamoy Syrup (page 119), for rim

Ice, for serving

2 ounces tequila blanco

2 ounces mango nectar

1 ounce elderflower liqueur (St-Germain)

½ ounce freshly squeezed lime juice

Orange Fanta, to top

This cocktail is inspired by childhood memories of mango Mexican candy and soda pop. My mouth waters whenever I think about Mexican chile–covered mango lollipops—the sweet and spicy flavors are an irresistible combination and are the foundation of this fun concoction. The addition of Pop Rocks and Fanta soda should have you feeling like a kid again.

▶ Mix together the Pop Rocks and Tajín seasoning to taste, and sprinkle on a saucer. Dip the rim of the glass in the chamoy syrup and then roll into the Tajín–Pop Rock mixture, coating the rim evenly. Fill the glass with ice, being careful not to mess up the rim. Add the tequila, mango nectar, elderflower liqueur, and lime juice to a shaker tin and shake vigorously. Strain into the glass and top with Fanta.

Mi Amor

Up

Tools: shaker, strainer, cocktail glass

2 ounces Rose Petal Tequila (page 111)

2 ounces passion fruit nectar

½ ounce raspberry liqueur (Chambord)

½ ounce freshly squeezed lime juice

2 to 3 dashes rose water

Fresh or dried edible rose petals, for garnish

From roses to passion fruit, this drink represents love in every ingredient, and it's a fitting drink for a romantic date night or anniversary dinner. Rose petal–infused tequila mixed with passion fruit nectar and silky raspberry liqueur and topped with a few dashes of rose water make this one of the loveliest cocktails in this book.

▸ Combine the tequila, passion fruit nectar, raspberry liqueur, and lime juice in a shaker tin and shake vigorously. Strain into the glass and top with the rose water and a sprinkle of dried rose petals for garnish.

Pom Pom

Rocks or Up

Tools: shaker, strainer, rocks or martini glass

Ice, for shaking and serving

2 ounces tequila blanco

2 ounces 100 percent pomegranate juice

1 ounce Pama pomegranate liqueur

1 ounce freshly squeezed lime juice

½ ounce Grenadine (page 117)

Pomegranate arils, for garnish

This recipe showcases all things pomegranate. The Pom Pom incorporates pomegranate juice, homemade grenadine (which is essentially pomegranate syrup), pomegranate liqueur, and a little bit of citrus. This cocktail could be served on the rocks or up in a martini glass.

► Combine the ice, tequila, pomegranate juice, pomegranate liqueur, lime juice, and grenadine in a shaker, and shake vigorously. Strain into an ice-filled glass or chilled martini glass and garnish with pomegranate arils.

TIP: Pama, which is pomegranate liquor, is available at most liquor stores. If you're having a hard time finding it, you can substitute elderflower liqueur or Chambord.

Dulce de Leche

Rocks

Tools: hammer, nail, saucepan, shaker, strainer, rocks glass

FOR THE DULCE DE LECHE

1 (14-ounce) can sweetened condensed milk

FOR THE COCKTAIL

Ice, for shaking

1½ ounces tequila reposado

½ ounce caramel liqueur (Bailey's Salted Caramel)

2 ounces sweetened condensed milk

Ground cinnamon, for garnish

Dulce de leche is a sweet, milk-based caramel popular throughout Latin America. It's used as an ingredient in cakes, cookies, and flan; as an ice cream topping; and, in this case, in a decadent dessert cocktail. Dulce de leche can be found in the Mexican section or baking aisle in most grocery stores, and it is also super easy to make on your own by simply slow-heating a can of sweetened condensed milk. If you love caramel, you'll love this caramel-inspired dessert cocktail.

TO MAKE THE DULCE DE LECHE

▸ Using a hammer and a clean nail, make two holes in the lid of a sweetened condensed milk can. Place the can upright in the saucepan. Pour in enough water to fill the pan until it reaches about three-quarters of the way up the can—don't fully submerge the can. Bring the water to a boil; then reduce the heat to low. Simmer for 3 to 4 hours. Add more water as it boils down to maintain the water level. The sweetened condensed milk will slowly thicken and turn a dark amber color. After 3 to 4 hours, remove the can from the pan and let it cool. Once cooled, pour the dulce de leche into a bowl and whisk away any lumps.

TO MAKE THE COCKTAIL

▸ Pour 1 teaspoon of dulce de leche into the bottom of your serving glass, making sure to spread some around the inside of the glass. Fill the glass with ice, then set aside. In a cocktail shaker filled with ice, combine the tequila, caramel liqueur, 1 teaspoon of dulce de leche, and 2 ounces of sweetened condensed milk. Shake vigorously. Strain into the ice-filled rocks glass. Garnish with a sprinkle of cinnamon.

It's Bananas!

Blended, Batch, Serves 4

Tools: blender, highball glass

6 ounces tequila reposado

3 cups milk

2 ounces banana liqueur (99 Bananas or Crème de Banana)

2 whole bananas

1 teaspoon agave syrup

Whipped cream, for garnish

Ground cinnamon, for garnish

Crushed banana chips, for garnish

Licuado is a popular Latin American drink made by blending fruit, milk, and ice into what resembles a smoothie. Banana licuados are similar to milkshakes but aren't as thick and have a frothy consistency. They are my absolute favorite, as they bring me back to childhood memories of living in Manhattan with my father, where we would often grab banana smoothies from a Mexican fruit shop by our apartment. This grown-up version is a wonderful way to pack some healthy potassium into your diet. Indulging in a little cocktail drinking with some fruity health benefits is multitasking at its finest.

▶ Pour the tequila, milk, banana liqueur, bananas, and agave syrup into a blender and blend until frothy. Pour into a highball glass and top with whipped cream. Garnish with a sprinkle of cinnamon and banana chip pieces.

TIP: Most liquor stores carry the 1-ounce mini bottle of 99 Bananas liqueur, so you don't have to commit to purchasing a whole bottle of banana liqueur for this recipe.

VARIATION TIP: If you prefer a thicker licuado, blend in 1 cup of ice or try using vanilla ice cream for more of a milkshake consistency. Other popular licuado flavors are papaya, strawberry, and peach.

Mexican-Style Cappuccino

Hot

Tools: cup, milk frother, coffee cup or mug

FOR THE KAHLÚA FOAM

3 tablespoons milk, cold

½ teaspoon Kahlúa

FOR THE CAPPUCCINO

1 ounce Coffee Tequila (page 110)

1 ounce coffee-flavored liqueur (Kahlúa or Mr. Black)

4 ounces freshly brewed coffee

Ground cinnamon, for garnish

My introduction to coffee cocktails was on my first skiing trip to Lake Tahoe, where Irish coffee was the main hit on the slopes. I enjoyed the warm whiskey cocktail so much that I ended up just people watching while sitting at the bar instead of actually going skiing. Once I realized there was a Mexican version of the Irish coffee that had tequila instead of whiskey, I was sold. In my typical foam-obsessed fashion, I've upgraded the classic Mexican coffee cocktail to a cappuccino version with Kahlúa-infused milk foam instead of oh-so-typical whipped cream.

TO MAKE THE KAHLÚA FOAM

▸ Pour the cold milk and Kahlúa into a cup; then whip with a milk frother and set aside.

TO MAKE THE CAPPUCCINO

▸ Pour the coffee tequila and liqueur into a coffee cup; then add the hot coffee. Top with 2 tablespoons of Kahlúa foam and a sprinkle of cinnamon.

VARIATION TIP: If you don't have a milk frother, substitute whipped cream for the foam. Add a few scoops of vanilla ice cream to make this a decadent, boozy dessert.

Hor-Chai-ta Martini

Up

Tools: saucepan, jigger, shaker, strainer, coupe or martini glass (chilled)

FOR THE HORCHATA-CHAI TEA (ENOUGH FOR 3 MARTINIS)

9 ounces rice milk

1 tea bag vanilla chai or regular chai

FOR THE MARTINI

2 ounces tequila reposado

1 ounce RumChata

Ice, for shaking

Ground cinnamon, for garnish

Horchata is a traditional sweet rice milk beverage that's beloved throughout Latin America. This cocktail combines the vanilla and cinnamon flavors of horchata with the bold flavors of chai, a combination that blends perfectly with the smoky, caramel flavor profiles in tequila reposado. This cocktail is a delicious dessert martini that can be enjoyed any time of the year.

TO MAKE THE HORCHATA-CHAI TEA

► In a saucepan over medium heat, bring the rice milk to a simmer. Steam 1 chai tea bag for every 9 ounces of rice milk. You can make this in large batches if you are planning to serve multiple drinks in one night. The horchata-chai tea can be stored in the refrigerator for 3 to 5 days.

TO MAKE THE MARTINI

► Pour the tequila, RumChata, and 3 ounces of horchata-chai tea into a shaker filled with ice. Shake vigorously until well chilled; then strain into a martini glass. Sprinkle with cinnamon.

VARIATION TIP: Use a premade horchata in place of the rice milk if you can find some locally. If you can't find RumChata, you can swap it for an almond- or vanilla cream–based liquor. You can also make this cocktail on the rocks with a cinnamon swizzle stick for garnish in place of the ground cinnamon. Take it up a notch by using coffee ice cubes instead of regular ice cubes in a rocks version to add a coffee-based twist.

La Vida Mocha

Up

Tools: coffee maker, martini glass, shaker, strainer

2 ounces freshly brewed coffee or espresso

1 teaspoon chocolate syrup, plus some for garnish

Ice, for shaking

1 ounce Coffee Tequila (page 110)

1 ounce coffee liqueur (Kahlúa or Mr. Black)

1 ounce heavy (whipping) cream or milk

Ground cinnamon, for garnish

This cocktail is all about livin' that mocha life. If you love coffee, chocolate, and tequila, this delicious after-dinner drink will be right up your alley. Get creative and decorate the inside of your martini glass with chocolate syrup to make a decadent, eye-catching cocktail.

▸ Brew a fresh cup of coffee or espresso and set it aside. Drizzle chocolate syrup around the inside of a chilled martini glass in random circular motions to create a beautiful chocolate design; then set aside. Fill a shaker tin with ice; then add the coffee tequila, coffee liqueur, brewed coffee, and cream. Shake vigorously until the shaker tin gets cold. Strain into your decorated martini glass and top with a sprinkle of cinnamon. The cream should form a slight foam on the top after straining.

VARIATION TIP: You can swap out the cinnamon garnish for espresso beans or chocolate shavings, whichever you have on hand. If you don't have time to infuse your tequila, just add ½ ounce more coffee liqueur to this recipe and deduct ½ ounce from the tequila measure.

Bloody Maria,
page 59

CHAPTER FOUR

Spicy and Savory

Tequini

Up

Tools: mixing glass, bar spoon, strainer, martini glass (chilled)

2½ ounces tequila blanco

½ ounce dry vermouth

1 dash aromatic bitters (Angostura or Peychaud)

Ice, for mixing

Olive, lemon twist, or pearl onion, for garnish

The tequini is the tequila variation of a classic gin martini. The dry vermouth and bitters help smooth out the tequila, allowing for easier sipping. Just like with classic gin martinis, the tequini works well garnished with an olive, pearl onion, or lemon peel. If you're making these for a party, impress your guests with a DIY martini bar where they can choose between different garnish and bitter options.

▸ Pour the tequila, dry vermouth, and bitters into a mixing glass filled with ice. Stir until chilled; then strain into a chilled martini glass. Garnish with an olive, lemon twist, or onion, whichever you prefer.

Rated R Martini

Up

Tools: mixing glass, bar spoon, strainer, martini glass (chilled)

Ice, for mixing

2 ounces tequila reposado

1 ounce dry vermouth

1 ounce olive brine

2 or 3 dashes Tabasco sauce

Stuffed olives (blue cheese, jalapeño, garlic), for garnish

2 dashes chili oil, for garnish

I'm a sucker for dirty martinis, but mostly because I love olives, especially ones stuffed with blue cheese. Adding extra olives to a martini is almost like having dinner in a glass. I've discovered my favorite dirty version is using tequila instead of vodka and giving it a kick of heat by adding Tabasco, chili oil, and an assortment of stuffed olives for the garnish. This combo is so good that I eventually started asking patrons who ordered dirty martinis if they wanted to try my "hot and dirty" version—and I would say about 99 percent of them loved it. I couldn't bring myself to name this cocktail the Hot & Dirty Martini, so I went with something a little bit more appropriate: the Rated R Martini.

▸ In a mixing glass filled with ice, combine the tequila, dry vermouth, olive brine, and Tabasco. Stir well. Strain into a chilled martini glass. Garnish with olives and chili oil.

Escabeche Martini

Up

Tools: mixing glass, bar spoon, strainer, coupe or martini glass (chilled)

Ice, for mixing

2 ounces tequila reposado

1 ounce Ancho Reyes Verde

½ ounce escabeche brine (from a can of carrot and jalapeño pickles)

1 dash chili or garlic-chili oil

Pickled jalapeño, for garnish

Pickled carrot, for garnish

Escabeche is the Spanish word for "pickle." It's also the name for the blend of jalapeños and carrots served alongside many Mexican dishes and is generally available as a garnish at restaurants or taco stands that have a salsa bar. Since pickle juice is a trending cocktail mixer these days, I thought that using escabeche brine would be a unique spin on both a dirty martini and a pickle juice cocktail.

▶ In a mixing glass filled with ice, combine the tequila, Ancho Reyes Verde, and escabeche brine. Stir well. Strain into a chilled coupe or martini glass. Garnish with a dash of chili oil and 2 or 3 pieces of pickled jalapeño and carrot.

Jalapeño Margarita

Rocks

Tools: rocks glass, rimmer, muddler, shaker, strainer

Kosher salt, for rim (optional)

Ice, for shaking and serving

6 jalapeño slices, divided

2 ounces Spicy Chile Pepper Tequila (page 112)

2 ounces freshly squeezed lime juice

1 ounce Ancho Reyes Verde

1 ounce Jalapeño Simple Syrup (page 115)

Lime wheel, for garnish

Almost every restaurant bar menu has some variation of a jalapeño margarita these days. Adding jalapeños to a margarita brings a fun, spicy spin to this traditional cocktail. The heat from the jalapeños paired with the sweet and sour mix is a wonderful flavor bomb that keeps you coming back sip after sip. Depending on your heat tolerance, you can make this slightly spicy with just a little bit of infused simple syrup or kick it way up by adding more jalapeños during the muddling process.

▸ Rim a rocks glass with cocktail salt (if using), fill with ice, and set aside. Muddle 3 slices of jalapeño with the tequila in a shaker tin. Add the lime juice, Ancho Reyes Verde, simple syrup, and ice to the shaker. Give a short shake to chill and incorporate the ingredients. Strain into the rimmed glass. Garnish with a lime wheel and the remaining jalapeño slices.

Hell's Bells

Rocks

Tools: knife, cutting board, rimmer, shaker, strainer

1 red bell pepper, refrigerated

Tajín, for rim

Ice, for serving

2 ounces tequila reposado

1 ounce Citrus Sour Mix (page 106)

1 ounce Jalapeño Simple Syrup (page 115)

½ ounce Ancho Reyes Verde

½ ounce vegetable juice (V8 or tomato juice)

3 or 4 cilantro sprigs, for garnish

You'll love cheers-ing with this cocktail's edible bell pepper cup. This recipe is a lighter take on a Bloody Mary, using a vegetable juice blend, fresh citrus, and muddled bell pepper. If you want more peppery, vegetal flavors, use green or red bell peppers; otherwise opt for yellow or orange bell peppers to have a sweeter, more aromatic cocktail.

TO MAKE THE BELL PEPPER CUP

▶ Slice off the top quarter of the bell pepper and set aside. Hollow out the inside of the larger portion of the bell pepper (this will be your glass). Remove the stem from the smaller piece and discard. Dice the leftover bell pepper into small chunks and place the diced pieces into a shaker tin.

TO MAKE THE COCKTAIL

▶ Dip your bell pepper cup into Tajín for the rim. The natural juices from the bell pepper should be enough for the Tajín to stick—if not, dip the bell pepper in honey or agave syrup first. Fill with ice and set aside. Muddle the tequila with the diced bell peppers. Add the citrus sour mix, simple syrup, Ancho Reyes Verde, and vegetable juice to the shaker and shake until chilled. Strain the liquid into the bell pepper cup. Garnish with cilantro.

VARIATION TIP: If you don't have Ancho Reyes Verde, substitute with orange liqueur. If you have a juicer on hand and want to go the extra bell pepper mile, use fresh bell pepper juice instead of the vegetable juice blend.

Bloody Maria

Rocks

Tools: shaker, strainer, pint glass

Salt or Tajín, for rim

Ice, for serving and shaking

2 ounces tequila añejo

5 ounces Bloody Mary Mix (page 108)

Lime wheel, for garnish

Stuffed olives (blue cheese, jalapeño, garlic), for garnish

Cilantro sprigs, for garnish

Celery rib, for garnish

Cornichons, for garnish

The Bloody Maria is a tequila version of the classic Bloody Mary. I prefer using tequila añejo or mezcal over vodka in Bloody Marys because the smoky, peppery notes in both of those spirits add more depth than vodka, which typically gets lost in the Bloody Mary mix. The secret to a good Bloody Mary is in the mix, and I have just the recipe for that.

▸ Rim a pint glass with salt or Tajín; then fill with ice and set aside. Add the tequila and Bloody Mary mix to a shaker filled with ice. Give a short shake and strain into a pint glass. Garnish with a lime wheel, olives, some cilantro, celery rib, or cornichons, as desired.

VARIATION TIP: Make this super spicy by using Spicy Chile Pepper Tequila (page 112) or muddle the tequila with jalapeños. You can also add a few dashes of your favorite hot sauce before mixing.

Get creative with your garnishes or set up a garnish bar so your guests can pick their own. Some of my favorites are bacon slices, celery ribs, cilantro, escabeche (pickled jalapeños and carrots), and sliced jalapeños.

Dante's Inferno

Rocks

Tools: kitchen torch or grill, rocks glass, rimmer, shaker, strainer

Sliced pineapple, for garnish

Cayenne powder or chili powder, for rim

Ice, for serving and shaking

2 ounces Spicy Chile Pepper Tequila (page 112)

2 ounces pineapple juice (freshly squeezed, if possible)

1 ounce Jalapeño Simple Syrup (page 115)

½ ounce Ancho Reyes

½ ounce Grenadine (page 117)

1 chile pepper (habanero, Thai, or jalapeño), for garnish

This is the ultimate spicy cocktail and one that's guaranteed to set your mouth on fire. Making the infused tequila and simple syrup will help you practice your craft cocktail skills. A little bit of pineapple juice helps bring down the heat (slightly), and a float of grenadine makes this cocktail look like a fiery flame. If you really like spice, you can take the heat level up by muddling the tequila with additional chile peppers and using a few dashes of your favorite hot sauce. Fair warning: If you do that, you may want to keep a glass of milk on hand for after the first few sips.

▸ Torch or grill the sliced pineapple and set aside. Half-rim a rocks glass with cayenne or chili powder, fill with ice, and set aside. Shake the tequila, pineapple juice, simple syrup, and Ancho Reyes in a shaker tin filled with ice. Strain into the prepared rocks glass and add a float of grenadine. Garnish with the charred pineapple and chile pepper.

Spicy Mango Margarita

Rocks

Tools: rocks glass, rimmer, shaker, muddler, strainer

Tajín, for rim

Ice, for serving and shaking

4 jalapeño slices, divided

2 ounces Spicy Chile Pepper Tequila (page 112)

2 ounces mango nectar

1 ounce orange liqueur (triple sec or Grand Marnier)

1/2 ounce Jalapeño Simple Syrup (page 115)

1/2 ounce freshly squeezed lime juice

Sliced mango, for garnish

Juicy sliced mangos sprinkled with lime juice and Tajín seasoning are a classic Mexican treat and a base for this delicious margarita. The mango nectar in this recipe helps bring down the heat of the chile-infused tequila and spicy simple syrup, creating an approachable spicy cocktail that won't be painful to drink.

▸ Rim the rocks glass with Tajin; then fill with ice and set aside. Muddle 2 or 3 jalapeño slices with the tequila in a shaker tin. Fill with ice and add the mango nectar, orange liqueur, simple syrup, and lime juice. Shake vigorously; then strain the mixture into the rimmed rocks glass. Garnish with fresh mango and the remaining jalapeño slices.

MANGO FAN: Peel and slice 1/2 of a mango; then stack the slices on top of one another. Use a cocktail pick to skewer the pieces together in the bottom portion of the stacked slices. Slowly spread the slices apart so they look like a fan.

SMOKING JALAPEÑO: Torch or grill jalapeño slices for a smoky finishing touch.

Avocado Margarita

Blended, Serves 2

Tools: margarita glasses, rimmer, blender

Chile-lime salt or Tajín, for rim

2 cups crushed ice

4 ounces tequila blanco

3 ounces freshly squeezed lime juice

2 ounces orange liqueur

1 teaspoon agave syrup

1 avocado, halved, pitted, and peeled

5 cilantro sprigs, plus more for garnish (optional)

2 lime wedges, for garnish

Really? Avocados in a margarita? Yes! The creamy consistency of blended avocado helps make a super smooth, luscious margarita. Orange liqueur and agave syrup help sweeten it up, creating a refreshing, savory cocktail that is perfect for summer.

▸ Rim margarita glasses with chile-lime salt or Tajín. Fill with ice and set aside. Combine the tequila, lime juice, orange liqueur, agave syrup, avocado, and cilantro (if using) in a blender and blend until smooth. Pour into the prepared margarita glasses. Garnish each glass with cilantro and a lime wedge.

VARIATION TIP: Make this margarita spicy by using Spicy Chile Pepper Tequila (page 112) and Jalapeño Simple Syrup (page 115) and adding a few slices of jalapeño before blending.

Green Machine

Rocks

Tools: blender, strainer
old-fashioned glass

2 ounces water

**1½ ounces tequila
blanco**

**1½ ounces freshly
squeezed lemon juice**

**1 ounce Agave-Ginger
Syrup (page 118)**

**½ ounce Ancho Reyes
Verde**

½ cup spinach

Ice, for serving

Microgreens, for garnish

**Edible flower, for
garnish (optional)**

Not too long ago, I was at a trendy vegan restaurant in Hollywood where I ordered a spinach lemonade to feel like I fit in with the "hip" crowd. I was pleasantly shocked at how delicious it was, plus the spinach was blended, so it created this frothy green foam that I loved. (Have I mentioned my foam obsession?) I figured I would try to re-create this delicious, healthy green concoction at home a few times a week to keep up with my daily servings of leafy greens. Well, my green juice "diet plan" lasted about a week until I figured out a surefire way to really keep up with the spinach juice intake: adding tequila.

▸ Blend the water, tequila, lemon juice, agave-ginger syrup, Ancho Reyes Verde, and spinach in a blender without ice. Strain into an old-fashioned glass filled with ice and garnish with microgreens and an edible flower (if using).

R&R Spa Water

Rocks

Tools: vegetable peeler, collins glass, muddler, shaker, strainer

1 cucumber

Ice, for serving and shaking

Pink peppercorns, for garnish

2 or 3 basil leaves, plus 1 sprig for garnish

1½ ounces tequila blanco

½ ounce elderflower liqueur (St-Germain)

½ ounce Lavender-Honey Syrup (page 116)

3 ounces cucumber soda or tonic water

Lemon slice, for garnish

Everyone needs a little bit of R&R (rest and relaxation) in their lives, but not everyone has the luxury of making it to the spa without breaking the bank. This cocktail has all the elements of the fancy, refreshing water that is usually served at spas. It has a little bit of cucumber and lemon, fresh basil, lavender syrup, and oh-so-relaxing tequila to help you bring that spa vibe right into your own kitchen.

► Create cucumber ribbons by pulling a vegetable peeler lengthwise down the cucumber. Place the ribbons in a collins glass in a spiral formation so they stick to the inside. Fill the glass with ice and pink peppercorns; then set aside. Muddle the basil leaves and tequila in a shaker tin. Fill the shaker with ice, the elderflower liqueur, and the lavender-honey syrup. Give it a short shake and strain over the prepared glass. Top with the cucumber soda water and garnish with a lemon slice and basil sprig.

Cucumber Bombs

Shooters, Makes 4

Tools: paring knife, cutting board, apple corer or small spoon, shaker, strainer

2 large cucumbers

Salt, for garnish

Tajín, for rim

**FOR THE
SHOOTER**

6 ounces tequila blanco

Ice, for shaking

**4 ounces orange liqueur
(Cointreau, triple sec,
or Grand Marnier)**

**2 ounces freshly
squeezed lime juice**

My friend made these amazing edible shot glasses out of cucumbers at a party one year, and I still think about them at least once a week. Prepping the little cucumber cups takes a bit of time, but they are so worth it. This will be your new favorite way to take tequila shots or shooters, guaranteed.

TO MAKE THE CUCUMBER SHOT GLASSES

▶ Cut each cucumber into 2-inch sections, making sure to cut a straight line on the top and bottom of each piece. Use an apple corer or small spoon to scoop out the center of the cucumber and reserve the flesh. Be sure to leave at least a ½ inch on the bottom of each cup to prevent any leaks. Sprinkle each cup with salt and then rim with Tajín and set aside.

TO MAKE THE SHOOTER

▶ Muddle the scooped-out cucumber flesh and tequila in a shaker tin. Add ice, orange liqueur, and lime juice and shake vigorously. Strain into the prepared cucumber shot glasses.

Carrot-Ginger Elixir

Rocks

Tools: peeler, shaker, strainer, old-fashioned or highball glass

1 carrot

Ice, for shaking and serving

1½ ounces tequila reposado

½ ounce orange liqueur (Grand Marnier, Cointreau, or triple sec)

½ ounce Agave-Ginger Syrup (page 118)

1 ounce carrot juice

Carrot and ginger are a classic, delicious pairing popular in soup and veggie juice blends, so it only makes sense to use them together in a savory cocktail. The ingredients in this recipe are so healthy that it tastes more like a health elixir than a cocktail. This one is great for springtime parties or an afternoon brunch.

▸ Peel the carrot lengthwise into long ribbons and set aside. Fill a shaker tin with ice and add the tequila, orange liqueur, agave-ginger syrup, and carrot juice. Shake vigorously. Strain into an ice-filled old-fashioned or highball glass. Garnish with the carrot ribbons.

VARIATION TIP: I love using ribbon garnishes, and they are best created with carrots or cucumbers. You can finish the ribbons in a few different ways:

▸ Wrap the ribbons around the inside of a glass before adding the cocktail.
▸ Roll them up into a tight spiral, which ends up looking like a rose.
▸ Fold them like an accordion and skewer them on a cocktail pick.

Holé Molé

Rocks

Tools: shaker, strainer, old-fashioned glass

1½ ounces mezcal

½ ounce orange liqueur (Cointreau, Grand Marnier, or triple sec)

½ ounce agave syrup

1 ounce freshly squeezed lime juice

1 teaspoon molé sauce

Ice, for serving

2 or 3 dashes of molé or chocolate bitters

Ground cinnamon, for garnish

Sesame seeds, for garnish

Star anise pod, for garnish

Not only is this cocktail super fun to say, it also includes another delicious ingredient native to Mexico. Molé is a traditional savory-sweet Mexican sauce that has more than 30 ingredients, but the base is basically dried chiles, smoky whole spices, and chocolate or cocoa powder. It is typically poured over chicken breasts or served over top of enchiladas. I came across molé bitters recently on one of my online shopping quests to find the most unique bitters out there. Since I am a fan of molé sauce, I was so excited to see it in cocktail bitter form and couldn't wait to use it in a drink recipe. The Holé Molé is essentially a savory molé margarita and could fit into the "dinner-in-a-glass" category.

► Combine the mezcal, orange liqueur, agave syrup, lime juice, and molé sauce in a shaker tin and shake vigorously. Strain into an ice-filled old-fashioned glass. Top with the molé or chocolate bitters and garnish with a sprinkle of cinnamon, sesame seeds, and a star anise pod.

TIP: Molé sauce is sold in most grocery stores and is typically found next to the salsa and enchilada sauce. The most popular molé sauce brand I have seen is called Doña Maria and comes in an 8-ounce glass jar.

Chipotle-Cocoa Martini (Mexican Chocolate Martini)

Up

Tools: kitchen grater, shaker, strainer, martini glass

Chili-chocolate bar (Lindt Chili Chocolate, for example)

1 ounce dark chocolate syrup, plus additional for garnish

1½ ounces tequila reposado

1 ounce chocolate liqueur (Godiva)

2 ounces heavy (whipping) cream or milk

Ice, for shaking

Ground cinnamon

Chipotle or chili powder

This deliciously rich and savory dessert martini is inspired by spicy chili-chocolate combinations popular throughout Mexico. Mexican chocolate is a prime example of this, as it usually features a blend of cinnamon, vanilla, almonds, and ground chiles.

► Using a kitchen grater, take the chili-chocolate bar and grate in a slow, even motion to create chocolate shavings; then set aside. Drizzle chocolate syrup in circular motions into a chilled martini glass and set aside. Pour the tequila, chocolate liqueur, 1 ounce of chocolate syrup, and heavy cream into a cocktail shaker filled with ice, sprinkle with cinnamon and chipotle powder, and then shake vigorously. Strain into the glass and garnish with the chocolate shavings.

TIP: Most grocery stores carry the Lindt Chili Chocolate bars in their candy aisle. Other chocolate brands have a spicy variety as well—I have seen some at Trader Joe's and Cost Plus World Market.

Smoked Chai,
page 79

Smoky and Earthy

Grilled Peach Sangria

**Rocks, Batch,
Serves 4 to 6**

Tools: grill, pitcher, lid or plastic wrap, wine glasses

3 medium peaches, pitted and sliced

1 (750-mL) bottle sweet white wine (Moscato, Gewürztraminer, or pinot grigio)

8 ounces peach nectar

4 ounces mezcal

3 ounces orange liqueur (Cointreau, Grand Marnier, or triple sec)

1 ounce Thyme Simple Syrup (page 114)

4 ounces pineapple juice

½ teaspoon ground cinnamon

8 thyme sprigs, divided

Ice, for serving

This smoky grilled peach sangria is a delicious punch-style drink perfect for both the warm summer grilling months and chilly, cozy winter nights by the fireplace. Combining ground cinnamon and thyme simple syrup with grilled peaches and smoky mezcal makes this white sangria a savory take on a typically sweet, fruit-forward classic.

► On a grill or grill pan over medium-high heat, grill the peach slices until char marks appear; then flip and repeat on each side. Let cool and transfer to a pitcher. Add the white wine, peach nectar, mezcal, orange liqueur, thyme simple syrup, and pineapple juice to the pitcher. Stir to combine the ingredients. Add the ground cinnamon and 4 thyme sprigs; then give a quick stir to incorporate. Cover the pitcher with a lid or plastic wrap and refrigerate for 2 hours or overnight. To serve, pour in ice-filled wine glasses. Make sure to include the grilled peaches that have been soaking in the sangria in each serving glass. Garnish each glass with a thyme sprig.

Grapefruit-Rosemary Martini

Up

Tools: muddler, shaker, strainer, martini glass, kitchen torch or lighter

Rosemary sprig

1½ ounces mezcal

Ice, for shaking

2 ounces ruby red grapefruit juice

1 ounce elderflower liqueur (St-Germain)

½ ounce Rose Petal Simple Syrup (page 115)

I've created many variations of a grapefruit-rosemary cocktail for just about every bar menu I've worked on. The two ingredients work well together and are lovely for any season. Grapefruit's refreshing tart flavor pairs beautifully with rosemary's earthy aromas and savory notes, which remind me of fresh garden herbs in the spring along with fall baking herbs. Rose petal simple syrup and elderflower liqueur add a slight touch of sweetness that helps balance out the smoky mezcal and savory-tart flavors from the grapefruit and rosemary.

▸ Peel off 2 or 3 rosemary leaves from the rosemary sprig and muddle them with the mezcal in a shaker tin. Fill the shaker with ice and pour in the grapefruit juice, elderflower liqueur, and rose petal simple syrup. Shake vigorously until the cocktail shaker is cold. Strain into a chilled martini glass. Using a kitchen torch or lighter, flame the rosemary sprig until it smokes and then extinguish. Garnish with the torched rosemary sprig.

Thyme After Thyme

Up

Tools: shaker, strainer, martini glass (chilled)

2 ounces mezcal

1½ ounces freshly squeezed lemon juice

½ ounce elderflower liqueur (St-Germain)

½ ounce Thyme Simple Syrup (page 114)

Ice, for shaking

Thyme sprig, for garnish

Time after time, I have used thyme to add earthy, sweet flavors to a cocktail. This recipe is perfectly balanced with a hint of smoky mezcal, a touch of floral from the elderflower liqueur, and a bit of tartness that finishes with a savory yet sweet thyme simple syrup that rounds it all out. A simple garnish of a thyme sprig works wonderfully for creating a rustic finishing touch that adds fresh, herb-garden vibes fitting for any savory cocktail. Use lemon thyme if you can find it to add more lemony notes to this recipe. If not, regular thyme will work fine.

▸ Combine the mezcal, lemon juice, elderflower liqueur, and thyme simple syrup in a shaker tin filled with ice. Give a short shake to chill and incorporate the ingredients. Strain into a chilled martini glass. Garnish with a thyme sprig.

It's My Jam

Rocks

Tools: shaker, jigger, strainer, rocks glass

2 ounces mezcal

¾ ounce freshly squeezed orange juice

½ ounce orange liqueur (Cointreau, Grand Marnier, or triple sec)

1 teaspoon orange marmalade

Ice, for shaking

Dash orange bitters

Flamed or smoked orange peel, for garnish

Jam has been used in cocktails for decades: the marmalade cocktail was first featured in the *Savoy Cocktail Book* by Harry Craddock, published in 1930. A little bit of orange marmalade combined with the burnt-orange aromas of the torched orange peel and smoky mezcal make this one of my favorite simple smoky cocktails.

▶ Combine the mezcal, orange juice, orange liqueur, and orange marmalade to a shaker tin filled with ice. Shake vigorously to break down the marmalade. Strain into a chilled rocks glass. Top with a dash of orange bitters and garnish with a flamed or smoked orange peel.

VARIATION TIP: Get creative by using your favorite jam. Any type of berry preserve would work wonderfully in this cocktail. Throw in a few fresh berries for garnish along with a piece of smoking rosemary and you'll have another jammin' cocktail.

Brûléed Paloma

Up

Tools: paring knife, cutting board, kitchen torch, shaker, strainer, martini glass (chilled)

1 grapefruit

Raw sugar, for brûléeing

2 ounces mezcal

½ ounce orange liqueur (Cointreau, Grand Marnier, or triple sec)

1 ounce ruby red grapefruit juice

Ice, for shaking

1½ ounces grapefruit soda (Jarritos or San Pellegrino)

This recipe is a smoky take on a classic paloma, which is usually made with tequila blanco and grapefruit soda. My grandmother used to make me brûléed grapefruit for breakfast all the time—I loved the sugary, caramelized crust that transformed the extremely tart grapefruit, which I normally didn't like. Fast-forward to adulthood, and whenever I'm working with grapefruit in cocktails, I try to caramelize it or add sugar to the recipe in some way. The smoky notes of mezcal blend wonderfully with the toasted, sugary notes of the brûléed grapefruit. This cocktail is a great accompaniment for a breakfast spread or for sipping at brunch.

TO BRÛLÉE THE GRAPEFRUIT

▸ Slice the grapefruit into ¼- to ½-inch-thick wheels and spread the slices out on a heat-resistant plate or sheet of aluminum foil. Sprinkle about 1 teaspoon of raw sugar over each slice, making sure to coat the entire wheel. Using the torch flame, heat the sugar until it's melted and starts to turn dark amber. You will get the best results if you move the torch quickly back and forth over the grapefruit instead of keeping it still on one area. This process goes quickly and is time-sensitive—once the sugar starts bubbling and smoking, it should be close to being done. Don't leave the flame on one area for too long; otherwise, it will burn.

TO MAKE THE COCKTAIL

▸ Combine the mezcal, orange liqueur, and grapefruit juice in a shaker tin filled with ice. Give a short shake to chill and incorporate the ingredients. Strain into a chilled martini glass. Top with the grapefruit soda. Garnish with the brûléed grapefruit.

TIP: Using a kitchen torch is the quickest and easiest way to brulee something, plus it's fun. No torch? Simply bake on high for about 5 minutes or use your oven's broiler. Make sure to keep an eye on the grapefruit while it's in the oven to keep it from burning. Let the grapefruit cool before serving.

Charred Piña

Rocks

Tools: skewers, kitchen torch or grill, shaker, old-fashioned glass, rimmer, muddler, strainer

6 grilled pineapple chunks, divided

Black Hawaiian sea salt, for rim (optional)

1½ ounces mezcal

Ice, for shaking and serving

2 ounces pineapple juice

½ ounce freshly squeezed lemon juice

½ ounce Agave-Ginger Syrup (page 118)

As soon as summer hits, people start grilling everything from meat to desserts, but the one thing that has year-round grilling potential is pineapple. This Charred Piña cocktail works wonderfully any time of the year, especially when paired with Hawaiian-inspired dishes like pineapple-chicken teriyaki. Charring pineapple caramelizes the sugars, making it a delicious pairing with smoky mezcal.

TO MAKE THE CHARRED PINEAPPLE

▸ Skewer the pineapple chunks and grill on each side until char marks are present, about 3 to 4 minutes per side. Remove from the heat and set aside. If you have a kitchen torch, you can also flame the pineapple until it caramelizes and starts to brown instead of using the grill.

TO MAKE THE COCKTAIL

▸ Rim half of an old-fashioned glass with black Hawaiian sea salt (if using), fill with ice, and set aside. In a shaker tin, first muddle 3 chunks of charred pineapple with the mezcal; then top with ice. Pour the pineapple juice, lemon juice, and agave-ginger syrup into the tin. Give it a short shake to chill and incorporate the ingredients. Strain into the rimmed glass. Garnish with a pick of charred pineapple chunks.

VARIATION TIP: Muddle with 2 or 3 slices of charred jalapeño and rim with Tajín instead of black sea salt.

Smoked Chai

Served hot or iced

Tools: mixing glass, shaker, mug, kitchen torch or lighter

1 bag chai tea

2 ounces tequila añejo

½ ounce Frangelico

½ ounce vanilla coffee creamer or milk

Ice (optional)

Cinnamon stick, for garnish

Chai is one of my favorite drinks because of its complex flavor profile—it's a little bit sweet and creamy mixed with toasty, aromatic baking spices. The cinnamon, cloves, and cardamom in chai pair nicely with the toasty notes of tequila añejo, making this cocktail a stellar smoky addition to your list of winter or after-dinner drink options. The smoking cinnamon stick garnish adds an extra impressive touch. I like to use a splash of vanilla coffee creamer instead of milk to mimic a vanilla chai latte.

TO MAKE THE COCKTAIL

▸ Steep a tea bag of your favorite brand of chai in hot water. Add the tequila, Frangelico, 3 ounces of hot chai, and vanilla coffee creamer to a mixing glass. Stir to incorporate the ingredients. Pour into a mug.

TO MAKE THE TORCHED CINNAMON STICK

▸ Using a kitchen torch or lighter, flame the cinnamon stick until it starts to smoke, but don't let it catch on fire. Garnish the drink with the cinnamon while it's still smoking.

VARIATION TIP: If you're a fan of coffee-chai lattes, you can easily make this a "dirty" chai version by using coffee ice
    This drink would also be delicious served on the rocks—just let the tea cool before mixing the drink and then pour over ice.

Bruja Blanca

Rocks

Tools: aluminum foil, shaker, rocks glass, muddler, jigger, strainer

1 chamomile tea bag

Dried sage leaves, for garnish

2 or 3 rosemary leaves

1½ ounces mezcal

Ice, for shaking and serving

½ ounce elderflower liqueur (St-Germain)

1 ounce Lavender-Honey Syrup (page 116)

1 ounce freshly squeezed lemon juice

1 or 2 dashes palo santo bitters

I have a few variations of a Witch Doctor cocktail that usually involve burning sage and incorporating holistic ingredients like lavender and palo santo bitters into the recipe. This Bruja Blanca cocktail is the mezcal variation of that (*bruja blanca* means "white witch" in Spanish). It will be just the remedy anytime you need to cleanse your personal space or have a calm evening.

▶ Steep a bag of chamomile tea in 6 ounces of hot water. Carefully light the dried sage on fire; then blow out quickly. Place the smoking sage on a piece of aluminum foil and turn the rocks glass upside down over the sage, trapping the smoke while it disperses. In a shaker tin, muddle the rosemary leaves with the mezcal, and then fill with ice. Pour in the elderflower liqueur, lavender-honey syrup, chamomile tea, and lemon juice. Give a short shake to chill and incorporate the ingredients. Flip the rocks glass back over and strain the shaker ingredients into the glass. Fill with ice and top with the palo santo bitters. Garnish with the freshly torched sage bunch.

Cilantro-Lime Margarita

Rocks

Tools: old-fashioned glass rimmer, muddler, shaker, jigger, strainer

Floral salt, for rim (page 103; optional)

Ice, for shaking and serving

Cilantro bunch, for muddling and garnish

4 to 6 coriander seeds

2 ounces tequila blanco

1 ounce orange liqueur (Cointreau, Grand Marnier, or triple sec)

2 ounces freshly squeezed lime juice

1 ounce Thyme Simple Syrup (page 114)

Lime wheel, for garnish

This recipe is my savory tequila version of the classic rum-based mojito. I love cilantro and use it in abundance when I cook Mexican food at home, but I know not everyone is a fan. If you enjoy cilantro, then you'll love this fresh herb-based margarita that partners well with Mexican food or warm summer days. Muddling cilantro leaves with coriander seeds (the seed of the cilantro plant) adds clean, crisp flavors of cilantro that complement the savory thyme simple syrup and tart lime juice. The floral salt garnish and bright green flecks of cilantro in the glass make this an especially eye-catching cocktail.

▸ Rim an old-fashioned glass with floral salt (if using), fill with ice, and set aside. Muddle a pinch of cilantro leaves and the coriander seeds with the tequila in a shaker tin. Add the orange liqueur, lime juice, thyme simple syrup, and ice to the shaker. Give a short shake to chill and incorporate the ingredients. Strain into the rimmed glass. Garnish with a lime wheel and cilantro.

Mezcal Aperol Spritz

Rocks

Tools: wine glass, bar spoon

2 ounces prosecco

2 ounces Aperol or Campari

1 ounce mezcal

1 ounce grapefruit soda

Ice, for serving

Torched orange peel, for garnish

The traditional Aperol spritz is a refreshingly light and bubbly low-ABV cocktail that's popular in Italy and is mostly consumed on hot summer days. Aperol is a dry, bitter aperitif with hints of burnt orange and rhubarb. Adding mezcal to this classic cocktail brings in earthy notes that work well with the bitterness of the Aperol. Torching the orange peel garnish mimics the burnt orange notes from the Aperol as well.

▸ Combine the prosecco, Aperol, mezcal, and grapefruit soda in a wine glass filled with ice. Give it a quick stir with a spoon. Serve with a torched orange peel.

Navidad

Up

Tools: kitchen torch or lighter, muddler, shaker, jigger, strainer, martini glass (chilled)

2 rosemary sprigs, divided

2 fresh cranberries, for garnish

2 ounces tequila añejo

Ice, for shaking

1/2 ounce orange liqueur (Cointreau, Grand Marnier, or triple sec)

1/2 ounce agave syrup

2 ounces cranberry juice

1/2 ounce orange juice

Ground cinnamon

This cocktail looks like Christmas in a glass and smells like it, too. During the fall and winter seasons, I tend to make homemade cranberry sauce. It's so good that I always wonder why I don't make it more throughout the rest of the year—the tart cranberry paired with fresh orange juice is so delicious that it makes perfect sense to put it in a cocktail! Garnished with fresh cranberries and a rosemary sprig, this cocktail will be a winner at your winter holiday party.

TO MAKE THE CRANBERRY-ROSEMARY GARNISH

▸ Pierce a rosemary sprig through the cranberries. This will create your cranberry pick. Using a kitchen torch or lighter, flame the rosemary until it smokes and then extinguish.

TO MAKE THE COCKTAIL

▸ Peel off 2 or 3 rosemary leaves from the remaining rosemary sprig and muddle them with the tequila in a shaker tin. Fill with ice and add the orange liqueur, agave syrup, cranberry juice, orange juice, and a sprinkle of cinnamon. Shake vigorously until the cocktail shaker is cold. Strain into a chilled martini glass. Garnish with the cranberry-rosemary pick.

TIP: Try to find rosemary with thick stems and use fresh cranberries whenever possible. Whole, frozen cranberries would also work, but they would need to be defrosted first.

Nuts for Mezcal

Rocks

Tools: jigger, mixing glass, bar spoon, strainer, rocks glass

1½ ounces mezcal

½ ounce Frangelico

2 or 3 dashes black walnut bitters (Fee Brothers)

Ice, for mixing and serving

Chopped roasted hazelnuts or roasted mixed nut blend, for garnish

Frangelico is a delicious hazelnut liqueur distilled from hazelnuts grown in the Piedmont region of Italy and blended with coffee, cocoa, and vanilla extracts. The sweet hazelnut flavors complement the earthy mezcal, and the black walnut bitters tie them both together, making this a delicious after-dinner drink.

▸ Combine the mezcal, Frangelico, and black walnut bitters in a mixing glass filled with ice. Stir until well chilled. Strain into a rocks glass filled with large ice cubes. Garnish with chopped roasted nuts.

The Beekeeper

Tools: kitchen torch or cocktail smoker, aluminum foil, martini glass, shaker, jigger, strainer

Dried lavender sprig, for garnish

1½ ounces tequila blanco

½ ounce elderflower liqueur (St-Germain)

1 ounce Lavender-Honey Syrup (page 116)

1 ounce freshly squeezed lemon juice

Ice, for shaking

This recipe is a fun, smoky twist on a traditional Bee's Knees cocktail. It includes honey and lemon juice like the classic but also incorporates lavender (a favorite flower of bees) and some smoke, which beekeepers use to calm bees while doing hive inspections.

▸ Carefully light the dried lavender sprig on fire; then blow it out quickly. Place the smoking sprig on a piece of aluminum foil and turn the martini glass upside down over the lavender to trap the smoke while it disperses. Combine the tequila, elderflower liqueur, lavender-honey syrup, and lemon juice in a shaker tin filled with ice. Give a short shake to chill and incorporate the ingredients. Flip the martini glass back over and strain the shaker ingredients into the glass. Garnish with the freshly torched lavender sprig.

VARIATION TIP: Make this in a larger batch and present the cocktail in a decanter filled with lavender smoke. You will need a medium-size decanter with a lid or stopper and a cocktail smoking tool with a flexible hose attachment. Pour the batched cocktail into a decanter. Use dried lavender pods in your cocktail smoker and insert the smoker hose into the decanter, being careful not to submerge it in the liquid. Fill the decanter up with lavender smoke and close the lid to trap the smoke inside. Swirl the decanter around to mix the smoke with the liquid. Pour into ice-filled martini glasses and garnish with a lavender sprig. Have fun smelling and watching the smoke disperse while you sip.

Toasted Coconut Margarita

Blended, Serves 2

Tools: skillet or baking sheet, 2 small plates, margarita glasses blender

Coconut flakes, for rim

Agave syrup or honey, for rim

3 ounces mezcal

2 ounces orange liqueur (Cointreau, Grand Marnier, or triple sec)

4 ounces cream of coconut (Coco Lopez or Real Coconut)

2 ounces freshly squeezed lime juice

4 ounces coconut milk

Ice, for blending

Lime wheel, for garnish

My favorite Mexican restaurant serves its coconut margaritas in large fishbowl glasses with a toasted coconut flake rim. It looks so delicious and tropical that it's hard to resist ordering one. For this recipe, I decided to use a smoky mezcal instead of tequila to complement the toasted coconut. If you can't find toasted coconut flakes at your local grocery store, they are very easy to make at home. I prefer toasting them myself anyway because they make my kitchen smell amazing and taste better than the premade version.

TO TOAST THE COCONUT FLAKES

▶ You can toast coconut on the stovetop or in the oven. For the stovetop, place the flakes in a large skillet. Cook over low-medium heat, stirring often, until the flakes are golden brown, approximately 5 to 10 minutes. Let cool. If you prefer to use your oven, spread the flakes on a baking sheet and bake for 5 to 10 minutes at 325°F. Make sure to remove them once they start browning so they don't burn.

TO MAKE THE MARGARITA

▶ Pour a little bit of agave syrup onto a small plate. Scatter a layer of toasted coconut flakes onto another small plate or piece of wax paper. Dip the rim of each glass into the agave syrup; then roll in the toasted coconut flakes so they stick to the glass.

▸ In a blender, combine the mezcal, orange liqueur, cream of coconut, lime juice, and coconut milk, and fill with ice. Blend until smooth. Slowly pour the cocktail into the center of the prepared glasses, being careful not to mess up the presentation. Garnish with a lime wheel.

TIP: Cream of coconut is not the same as coconut milk or coconut cream. Make sure you are using the right product. Typically, cream of coconut is located in the cocktail mixer section of the store.

The Cosmos,
page 94

Dry and Sour

La Diabla

Rocks

Tools: highball glass

1½ ounces tequila reposado

½ ounce freshly squeezed lime juice

Ice, for serving

3 ounces ginger beer

½ ounce raspberry liqueur (Chambord)

2 raspberries, for garnish

Candied ginger, for garnish

La Diabla is my elegant riff on the classic El Diablo that was first referenced as the Mexican El Diablo in *Trader Vic's Book of Food and Drink*, published in 1946. The original El Diablo recipe consists of tequila, lime juice, crème de cassis (a sweet blackcurrant liqueur), and ginger beer. Since crème de cassis is hard to find, I've swapped it with the queen of all berry liqueurs, Chambord, which is readily available at most grocery or liquor stores. *La diabla* translates to "she-devil" in Spanish, so it's the perfect name for this beautiful, sinfully delicious cocktail.

▸ Pour the tequila and lime juice into a highball glass filled with ice. Top with the ginger beer. Finish with a float of Chambord. Garnish with a cocktail pick speared with two raspberries and a piece of candied ginger.

Ranch Water

Rocks

Tools: highball glass

Ice, for serving

2 ounces tequila blanco

1 ounce freshly squeezed lime juice

Sparkling mineral water (such as Topo Chico), chilled

Lime wheel, for garnish

This contemporary highball cocktail hails from Texas. It's said to have originated from cattle workers in West Texas who wanted a refreshing cocktail to enjoy during the summer heat. Made with tequila, lime juice, and sparkling mineral water, it's the perfect fizzy drink to help cool off after a long day of hard work.

▶ Fill a highball glass with ice. Add the tequila and fresh lime juice. Top with sparkling water. Garnish with a fresh lime wheel.

Turbo Shandy

Straight

Tools: pint glass, rimmer

Tajín, for rim

6 ounces Mexican lager,
like Pacifico or Modelo

1½ ounces tequila
reposado

6 ounces Limeade
(page 107)

Lime wheel, for garnish

The shandy is a classic summertime beer-based cocktail that is equal parts beer and lemonade or lemon soda. We're going to amp it up with the addition of tequila and a Tajin rim, hence the name Turbo Shandy. I've swapped out lemonade with limeade because lime pairs better with tequila and Mexican lager. This is my go-to cocktail for relaxed day drinking or hangover cures.

▸ Rim a pint glass with Tajin. Pour the beer, tequila, and limeade into the glass. Garnish with a lime wheel.

The Siesta

Tools: shaker, strainer, martini glass (chilled)

2 ounces tequila blanco

½ ounce Campari

½ ounce freshly squeezed grapefruit juice

½ ounce freshly squeezed lime juice

½ ounce Simple Syrup (page 114)

Ice, for shaking

Grapefruit peel or lime wheel, for garnish

The Siesta is a modern classic created in 2006 by New York mixologist Katie Stipe. It is a refreshing mix of tequila, Campari, grapefruit juice, and lime juice. Campari is a bitter rhubarb-and-orange-flavored liqueur that pairs wonderfully with the earthy notes of tequila blanco and tart, aromatic grapefruit juice.

▸ Pour the tequila, Campari, grapefruit juice, lime juice, and simple syrup into an ice-filled shaker tin. Shake vigorously until the outside of the shaker is very cold, about 20 seconds. Strain into a chilled martini glass. Garnish with a grapefruit peel or lime wheel.

The Cosmos

Up

Tools: shaker, strainer, martini glass (chilled)

1½ ounces tequila blanco

1 ounce orange liqueur (Cointreau or Grand Marnier)

½ ounce freshly squeezed lime juice

1 ounce cranberry juice

½ teaspoon edible glitter

Ice, for shaking

Lime wedge, for garnish

This sparkly take on a cosmopolitan is out of this world—hence its name. The classic cosmopolitan is a tart vodka-based martini with cranberry juice, orange liqueur, and a squeeze of lime. To make our tequila version truly intergalactic, we're going to use edible glitter, or luster dust, to add eye-catching sparkle to this refreshingly tart martini.

▸ Combine the tequila, orange liqueur, lime juice, cranberry juice, and edible glitter in a shaker tin filled with ice. Shake until well chilled. Strain into a chilled martini glass. Garnish with a lemon slice.

TIP: Edible glitter can be found online or at specialty bake-shops. Opt for a silver or red glitter to blend well in this cocktail. You can also get cocktail glitter online that would work in this recipe, but it tends to be more expensive and harder to find.

Tagroni

Rocks

Tools: mixing glass, jigger, bar spoon, strainer, rocks glass

1 ounce tequila blanco

1 ounce Campari

1 ounce sweet vermouth

Ice, for mixing and serving

1 expressed orange peel, for garnish

The Negroni is a classic gin-based cocktail with equal parts gin, Campari, and sweet vermouth. It has had a resurgence in popularity in today's modern craft cocktail world. There's even an annual Negroni Week, challenging bartenders to come up with different takes on the classic recipe. The crisp, earthy flavors of tequila blanco pair wonderfully with bitter Campari in this recipe, and the combination is balanced out with sweet vermouth.

▸ Pour the tequila, Campari, and sweet vermouth into a mixing glass filled with ice. Stir until well chilled. Strain into a rocks glass filled with large ice cubes. Garnish with an expressed orange peel.

Reposado Old-Fashioned

Rocks

Tools: mixing glass, muddler, jigger, bar spoon, strainer, old-fashioned glass

1 Bing cherry, pitted and cut in half

1 orange slice

Ice, for mixing

3 ounces tequila añejo

½ ounce agave syrup

3 dashes Angostura bitters

4 dashes orange bitters

1 expressed orange peel, for garnish

The old-fashioned is a classic whiskey-based cocktail using sugar and bitters with a cherry and orange peel garnish to help mellow out the high-proof spirit. There is intense debate on whether cherries and oranges should be muddled in a real old-fashioned, with some noting that muddling the fruit is only popular in the United States. For this tequila-inspired old-fashioned, I call for muddling an orange slice and a fresh Bing cherry instead of an overly sugary maraschino cherry. The juice of the muddled fruit softens the tequila reposado, and using agave syrup instead of regular syrup complements the agave-based tequila. The addition of orange bitters adds extra citrusy aromas to be enjoyed with each sip.

▸ Muddle the cherry and orange slice in a mixing glass; then discard any whole chunks, making sure to keep the muddled juice in the glass. Fill the mixing glass halfway with ice; then pour in the tequila, agave syrup, Angostura bitters, and orange bitters. Stir for at least 30 seconds, making sure to dissolve the agave syrup. Strain into an ice-filled old-fashioned glass. Garnish with an expressed orange peel.

Jalisco Mule

Rocks

Tools: copper mug, jigger, bar spoon

1½ ounces tequila blanco

1 ounce Agave-Ginger Syrup (page 118)

6 ounces ginger beer

½ ounce freshly squeezed lime juice

Ice, for serving

Mint sprig, for garnish

Candied ginger, for garnish

Jalisco is a state in western-central Mexico and is the official birthplace of tequila. The Jalisco mule is a tequila take on the classic copper mug Moscow mule, which consists of vodka, lime juice, and ginger beer. This Jalisco mule incorporates agave-ginger syrup, which goes well with the tequila blanco, and calls for candied ginger as the garnish, which adds a fun, unique spin on a basic lime wheel garnish. I suggest using an intensely flavored ginger beer like Gosling's, Bundaberg, or Cock-N-Bull, since some other brands tend to be overly sweet with subtle ginger notes that end up falling flat in cocktails.

▸ Pour the tequila, agave-ginger syrup, ginger beer, and lime juice into a copper mug filled with ice. Stir to combine and dissolve the agave syrup. Garnish with a mint sprig and candied ginger.

Tamarind Sour

Rocks

Tools: mixing glass, shaker, strainer, rocks glass

1 tablespoon tamarind paste

1 tablespoon hot water

1½ ounces tequila reposado

1 ounce lemon juice, freshly squeezed

½ ounce agave syrup

Ice, for shaking and serving

Lemon wheel, for garnish

Agua de tamarindo **is a popular beverage throughout Latin America that looks similar to iced tea. Tamarind is a pod that is grown on its namesake trees and is widely used in a variety of different dishes. Its sweet and sour flavor makes it a great choice for a tequila sour cocktail playing on the influence of agua de tamarindo. Tamarind is known to be high in antioxidants and full of nutrients, so you may want to make a big batch of the tamarind juice to keep on hand for after a night of cocktail consumption.**

▶ In a mixing glass, mix the tamarind paste with the hot water and let cool. Pour the tequila, lemon juice, tamarind-water mixture, and agave syrup into a shaker tin filled with ice. Give a short shake to incorporate the ingredients. Strain into a rocks glass filled with ice. Garnish with a lemon wheel.

TIP: Tamarind is usually available in the Asian or Mexican section at grocery stores in the form of a powder, paste, or concentrate. If it's not at your local grocery store, it can easily be found in Asian, Latin, or Middle Eastern markets.

Kumquat Margarita

Rocks

Tools: shaker, muddler, old-fashioned glass

4 kumquats, divided

2 ounces tequila añejo

Ice, for shaking and serving

1 ounce kumquat liqueur or orange liqueur

1 ounce Citrus Sour Mix (page 106)

½ ounce agave syrup

A kumquat is a small citrus fruit about one inch in length that is very tart and has an edible rind. Most people just pop the whole thing into their mouth instead of peeling it. It tastes similar to a tangerine and is sourer than an orange, making it the perfect citrus fruit for a tart margarita. The kumquat liqueur in this recipe is available at most liquor stores. It is also a fantastic alternative to the orange liqueur used in many cocktail recipes.

► Muddle 2 whole kumquats with the tequila in a shaker tin; then fill with ice. Add the kumquat liqueur, citrus sour mix, and agave syrup. Shake vigorously until well chilled. Strain into an ice-filled old-fashioned glass. Garnish with the remaining 2 kumquats, speared on a toothpick.

Hoppy Sour

Rocks

Tools: shaker, strainer, rocks glass

2 ounce tequila blanco

1 ounce freshly squeezed grapefruit juice

½ ounce pamplemousse liqueur

½ ounce IPA Syrup (page 113)

Ice, for shaking and serving

3 dashes grapefruit or orange bitters

Flamed grapefruit peel, for garnish

If you love IPAs, this cocktail is for you. This tequila sour showcases tons of bittersweet hop flavor from the IPA syrup and pamplemousse liqueur. IPAs are known for their overly citrus, bitter flavor profiles, and the crisp pine notes complement the clean, earthy flavors of tequila blanco. Next time you're craving an IPA, try out this lovely cocktail instead.

▸ Pour the tequila, grapefruit juice, pamplemousse liqueur, and IPA syrup into a shaker tin filled with ice. Give a short shake to incorporate the ingredients. Strain into a rocks glass filled with ice. Garnish with a flamed grapefruit peel.

TIP: Pamplemousse liqueur is made from pink grapefruit. There are a few brands of pamplemousse liqueur available at most liquor stores, including Giffard and St. Elder.

Piña Sour

Up

Tools: shaker, strainer, martini glass (chilled), toothpick or fork

2 ounces Pineapple Tequila (page 110)

2 ounces pineapple juice (freshly squeezed, preferably)

1 ounce lemon juice

½ ounce pineapple liqueur

½ ounce Agave-Ginger Syrup (page 118)

Ice, for shaking

3 drops aromatic bitters, for decorative garnish (Angostura or Peychaud)

My favorite sour cocktail recipes are based on the foamy, egg-white version of a traditional whiskey sour. Pineapple sours are a great choice for creating eggless foam because pineapple juice naturally froths when shaken in a cocktail. This is a tequila variation of a traditional whiskey sour, featuring decorative designs using brightly colored aromatic bitters. This sour is best served in either a martini glass, coupe glass, or Nick & Nora glass.

▸ Pour the tequila, pineapple juice, lemon juice, pineapple liqueur, and agave-ginger syrup into an ice-filled shaker tin. Shake vigorously for 20 seconds. Strain into a chilled martini glass, making sure to create a frothy head when straining. Drip the bitters down in the center of the glass on top of the foam. Take a toothpick or fork and drag a line through the middle of the bitter dots to create a heart design in the foam.

TIP: Most of the foam will come out at the end of straining your drink, so it helps if you jiggle the shaker tin at the end to help aerate the final drops that come out of the strainer. This will help create a thicker foam layer on top.

There are different brands of pineapple liqueur available at grocery stores and liquor stores. Some of the popular brands I've seen are 99 Pineapple, Alizé Pineapple, or Giffard Caribbean Pineapple. A bottle of pineapple liqueur would be a great addition to your home bar for use in pineapple margaritas along with various tropical tiki drink recipes.

Cherry Limeade Crush

Rocks

Tools: highball glass, bar spoon

2 ounces tequila blanco

1 tablespoon Grenadine (page 117)

1 ounce freshly squeezed lime juice

Crushed ice, for serving

Lemon-lime soda (Sprite or 7-Up)

Lime wheel, for garnish

Maraschino cherries, for garnish

Sonic Drive-In's iconic Cherry Limeade was a special childhood treat for me every summer when visiting my grandparents. There were Sonics all over Texas, where they lived, while we only had a few scattered throughout back home in Los Angeles. This recipe is the sophisticated adult version, with tequila, homemade grenadine, and freshly squeezed lime juice poured over crushed ice and topped with as many maraschino cherries as your little heart desires.

▶ Pour the tequila, grenadine, and lime juice into a highball glass filled with crushed ice. Top with the lemon-lime soda. Give it a quick stir to incorporate the ingredients. Garnish with a lime wheel and maraschino cherries.

Remember Me

Rocks

Tools: rimmer, rocks glass, shaker, strainer

1 cup coarse salt

1 cup edible dried flower petals

Ice, for shaking and serving

2 ounces silver tequila

1 ounce elderflower liqueur

1 ounce freshly squeezed tangerine juice

1 marigold flower, stem removed, for garnish

This cocktail is inspired by one of my favorite holidays, Día de los Muertos. It incorporates the marigold flower that adorns altars and gravesites throughout the holiday celebrations. The marigold is known as the "flower of the dead" and is believed to attract the souls of the dead home with its aromatic scent and vibrant colors. The combination of the edible marigold, elderflower liqueur, and floral salt used in this recipe adds a beautiful touch that's fitting for toasting to fond memories of your own loved ones who have passed.

TO MAKE FLORAL SALT

► Combine the coarse salt and dried flower petals, and store in an airtight container. Edible-grade dried flower petals are readily available on Amazon.

TO MAKE THE COCKTAIL

► Rim a rocks glass with the floral salt and fill with ice. Combine the tequila, elderflower liqueur, and tangerine juice in a shaker filled with ice. Shake lightly until chilled; then strain into the center of the rimmed glass, being careful to not mess up the salt. Garnish with the marigold flower.

Iced tea spiked with Hibiscus Tea Tequila, page 111

Syrups, Mixers, and Staples

Citrus Sour Mix

Makes 6 cups

Tools: saucepan, wooden spoon, pitcher

2 cups water

1 cup agave syrup

2 cups freshly squeezed lemon juice

1 cup freshly squeezed lime juice

½ cup freshly squeezed orange juice

Sweet and sour mix is a bar staple that's used in a variety of cocktails. This citrus sour mix is a healthier version of a typical sweet and sour mix, incorporating three types of citrus instead of using only lime juice. Adding a little bit of lemon and orange juice creates a more complex, naturally sweeter version that uses less sugary syrup and relies more on the naturally sweet flavors of the different fruit. Since we are working with tequila and mezcal in these cocktails, I've used agave syrup instead of simple syrup to complement the agave-based spirit.

▸ Bring the water to a boil in a small saucepan over medium-high heat. Add the agave syrup and stir until dissolved. Remove the saucepan from the heat and let cool to room temperature. Pour the agave syrup mixture, lemon juice, lime juice, and orange juice into a large pitcher. Stir to incorporate all the ingredients. Store in the refrigerator for up to 5 days.

Limeade

Makes 4 cups

Tools: saucepan, wooden spoon, pitcher

2 cups water

1 cup agave syrup

2 cups freshly squeezed lime juice

Limeade is simply the lime version of lemonade. For this recipe, we're going to be using agave syrup instead of simple syrup, which is typically used in lemonade, along with lime juice and water to make this refreshingly tart beverage.

▸ Bring the water to a boil in a small saucepan. Add the agave syrup and stir until dissolved. Remove the saucepan from the heat and let cool to room temperature. Pour the syrup mixture and lime juice into a large pitcher. Stir to incorporate all the ingredients. Store in the refrigerator for up to 5 days.

Bloody Mary Mix

Tools: blender, airtight container

5 cups tomato juice or vegetable juice blend (such as V8)

3 ounces lime juice, freshly squeezed

2 ounces orange juice, freshly squeezed

1 ounce olive brine (optional)

1 tablespoon celery salt

1 teaspoon Worcestershire sauce

1 teaspoon horseradish (optional)

1 teaspoon freshly ground black pepper

3 or 4 dashes Tabasco or Tapatío sauce (optional)

There are a ton of variations of Bloody Mary mix, and almost every bartender claims that they have the "best" mix recipe, with their own secret ingredients or ratios. I prefer to use vegetable juice blends over straight tomato juice as the base and include a little bit of olive brine and orange juice to add some complex flavors. Horseradish is an ingredient that not everyone likes, so feel free to omit it if you aren't a fan. If you like your Bloody Mary extra spicy, add a few more dashes of hot sauce or throw in a few slices of jalapeño before blending.

▸ Blend the tomato juice, lime juice, orange juice, olive brine (if using), celery salt, Worcestershire sauce, horseradish (if using), pepper, and Tabasco until all the ingredients are thoroughly combined. Store in an airtight container in the refrigerator for up to 4 days.

Tequila Infusions

Infusion tools: airtight glass container that will hold at least 4 cups, glass bottle that will hold at least 4 cups, funnel, mesh strainer or coffee filter

I absolutely love infusing tequila with fruit, herbs, coffee beans, or spices to add extra depth to my cocktails. The heightened flavors imparted to the tequila add complexity to drinks that you can't get from mixers or liqueurs alone. The basic tools needed for infusing are a large glass container with a lid, a storing bottle, a funnel, and time. I've listed in-depth recipes for the infusions we use in this book, but I encourage you to come up with your own combinations as well.

DRINK YIELD: These recipes call for a 750-mL bottle of tequila, which is roughly 25 ounces. Most of the recipes in this book call for 1½ to 2 ounces of tequila per recipe, so you should get more than 10 cocktails out of each batch.

Strawberry Tequila

1 (750-mL) bottle tequila blanco

1 (16-ounce) package strawberries, sliced, tops removed

► Pour the tequila into the airtight storage container and add the sliced strawberries. Give it a good shake to mix everything together. Store in your pantry or on your countertop (making sure they are not in direct sunlight) for 3 days, or until the strawberries look pale or white from their color being extracted. Using a funnel with a thin tip or a mesh strainer, strain the tequila into your final serving bottle, discarding the strawberries. Store in the refrigerator or on a shelf for up to 6 months.

CONTINUED →

Pineapple Tequila

1 (750-mL) bottle tequila blanco

1 whole pineapple, chopped, skin removed

▸ Pour the tequila into the airtight storage container and add the pineapple. Give it a good shake to mix everything together. Store in your pantry or on your countertop (making sure they are not in direct sunlight) for 3 days, or until the pineapple chunks look pale or white from their color being extracted. Using a funnel with a thin tip or a mesh strainer, straining the tequila into your final serving bottle, discarding the pineapple pieces. Store in the refrigerator or on a shelf for up to 6 months.

Coffee Tequila

1 (750-mL) bottle tequila blanco

2 cups coffee beans

▸ Pour the tequila into the airtight container and add the coffee beans, making sure to cover the coffee beans so they are fully submerged. Store for 3 days in a cool, dark place, like your kitchen pantry or a cabinet. Give the container a light shake every 1 or 2 days to agitate the coffee beans for better flavor extraction. After the third day of soaking, strain the tequila into your final serving bottle using a funnel or mesh strainer and discard the coffee beans. Store in the refrigerator or on a shelf for up to 6 months.

Hibiscus Tea Tequila

1 (750-mL) bottle tequila blanco

4 bags hibiscus tea blend (my favorite brand is Celestial Raspberry Zinger)

▸ Pour tequila into the airtight container and add tea bags. Let steep on your countertop (making sure it's not in direct sunlight) for 3 days, shaking once per day. After the third day of soaking, strain the tequila into your serving bottle using a funnel or mesh strainer, discarding the tea bags. Store in the refrigerator or on a shelf for up to 1 year.

Rose Petal Tequila

1 (750-mL) bottle tequila blanco

4 ounces edible tea-grade dried rose petals

▸ Pour tequila into the airtight container and add dried rose petals. Let steep on your countertop (making sure it's not in direct sunlight) for 3 days, shaking once per day. After the third day of soaking, strain the tequila into your serving bottle using a funnel or mesh strainer. Store in the refrigerator or on a shelf for up to 1 year. Edible tea-grade dried rose petals are available on Amazon and in some natural food markets.

CONTAINER TIPS

The large airtight container for infusing should hold at least 4 cups, enough for a 750-mL bottle along with the infusion ingredients. A mason jar or a glass pitcher with a spout works well. The glass bottle that the finished infused tequila is stored in should be able to hold at least 750 mL. I usually use the original tequila bottle for this, but I've also found really neat glass bottles with stoppers at the Dollar Store or online.

CONTINUED →

Spicy Chile Pepper Tequila

1 (750-mL) bottle tequila blanco

2 jalapeños, sliced, seeds removed

1 Thai chile pepper, sliced, seeds removed

½ habanero, sliced, seeds removed

► You will want to use latex or plastic gloves to prep this infusion. There is nothing worse than touching your eyes with your fingers after cutting up spicy peppers! Pour the tequila into the airtight container and add the jalapeños, Thai chile pepper, and habanero. The peppers are light, so they will probably float on top. Give the container a good shake to mix the peppers with the tequila. This infusion is pretty quick and will only need to soak for 10 to 12 hours, unless you want it really spicy—then 24 hours will do the trick. When you're happy with the spice level of the tequila, strain it into your final serving bottle using a funnel or mesh strainer and discard the peppers. Store in the refrigerator or on a shelf for up to 6 months.

HOW LONG WILL THEY LAST?

Alcohol is a natural preservative that inhibits bacterial growth, so these infusions are shelf-stable and will last for at least six months, depending on how you store them. As long as you are completely submerging your infusion ingredients in the alcohol while you are infusing them, you will prevent bacteria from growing in your concoction. Make sure to not leave any bits or pieces of the infusion ingredients exposed to air during the soaking process. If I know I am going to use the infusion batch pretty quickly, I will store it on my back bar to show off my infusion skills. If I know I will have one of the infusions for a few months, I will store it in the fridge and give it monthly smell and taste checks to ensure quality.

IPA Syrup

Tools: saucepan, wooden spoon, squeeze bottle or jar

1 (12-ounce) can IPA beer

1½ cups sugar

IPA syrup is one of my favorite cocktail syrups. It's a smoother, caramelized version of a typical IPA, packed full of all of the bitter citrus, floral, and pine flavors that make this variety of beer so popular. Heating equal parts beer and sugar on a stovetop and simmering the mixture down to a thick reduction creates this velvety, bittersweet syrup.

▸ Pour the IPA into a large saucepan over medium-high heat. Stir every couple minutes, until the IPA begins to boil. Once boiling, reduce the heat to a gentle simmer. Add the sugar and stir until it has dissolved, continuing to stir every 3 to 4 minutes for 30 to 45 minutes to prevent burning while reducing the liquid to a syrup consistency. Once cooled, transfer the syrup to a squeeze bottle or jar and store in the refrigerator for up to 4 weeks.

Simple Syrups

Simple syrup is a sweet, sugar-water syrup featured in many cocktail recipes. Using a sugar syrup in cocktails works better than plain granulated sugar because it's in liquid form and blends quickly and easily with other liquid ingredients. Sugar granules, on the other hand, take forever to dissolve and tend to sink to the bottom of a cocktail. Simple syrup is the base for many flavored cocktail syrups as well. When you make a flavored cocktail syrup, you are essentially creating an infused simple syrup. Here is a recipe for regular simple syrup, along with the flavored simple syrups used throughout this book.

Simple Syrup

Tools: saucepan, wooden spoon, airtight container or squeeze bottle

1 cup water

1 cup sugar

▸ Combine the water and sugar in a saucepan over medium-high heat. Bring to a boil, stirring, until the sugar has dissolved. Remove from the heat and allow the syrup to cool to room temperature. Transfer to an airtight container or store in a squeeze bottle for easy use. Store in the refrigerator for up to 4 weeks.

Thyme Simple Syrup

Tools: saucepan, wooden spoon, airtight container or squeeze bottle

1 cup water

1 cup sugar

5 thyme sprigs

▸ Combine the water and sugar in a saucepan over medium-high heat. Bring to a boil. Add the thyme sprigs to the saucepan and simmer for about 15 minutes. Stir until the sugar is dissolved. Remove the syrup from the heat, remove the thyme sprigs, and let the syrup cool to room temperature. Transfer to an airtight container or squeeze bottle for easy use. Store in the refrigerator for up to 4 weeks.

Jalapeño Simple Syrup

Tools: saucepan, wooden spoon, airtight container or squeeze bottle

1 cup water

1 cup sugar

1 jalapeño, sliced, seeds removed

▸ Combine the water and sugar in a saucepan over medium-high heat. Bring to a boil. Add the sliced jalapeño to the saucepan and simmer for about 15 minutes. Stir until the sugar is dissolved. Remove the syrup from the heat, remove the jalapeño slices, and let the syrup cool to room temperature. Transfer to an airtight container or squeeze bottle for easy use. Store in the refrigerator for up to 4 weeks.

Rose Petal Simple Syrup

Tools: 2 saucepans, wooden spoon, coffee filter or mesh strainer, airtight container or squeeze bottle

1 cup water

2 ounces edible tea-grade dried rose petals

1 cup sugar

½ cup rose water

▸ In a medium saucepan, bring the water to a boil over medium-high heat. Stir in the dried rose petals and reduce the heat to a simmer for 15 minutes. Remove from the heat and let cool to room temperature. Using a coffee filter or mesh strainer, strain the dried rose petals from the water, transferring the rose-infused water to another saucepan. Bring the water back up to a boil. Add the sugar to the boiling water and stir until it dissolves completely. Once dissolved, remove the saucepan from heat. Add the rose water and stir to blend all the ingredients. Let the syrup cool to room temperature; then transfer to an airtight container or squeeze bottle for easy use. Store in the refrigerator for up to 4 weeks.

Lavender-Honey Syrup

Tools: saucepan, wooden spoon, coffee filter or mesh strainer, airtight container or squeeze bottle

1 cup water

1 tablespoon dried lavender pods

1½ cups honey

Honey is a great sweetener alternative in cocktails, but it's a bit too thick to use straight out of a jar. Diluting it down with hot water makes for a thinner syrup that mixes well in many cocktail recipes. Honey syrup is most well known as a main ingredient in the classic Bee's Knees cocktail. This recipe takes it up a notch by infusing it with lavender pods to create a delicious aromatic lavender-honey syrup.

▶ In a medium saucepan, bring the water to a boil over medium-high heat. Stir in the dried lavender pods, reduce the heat, and let the mixture simmer for 15 minutes. Add the honey and stir until it has fully dissolved. Remove the pan from the heat and let it cool to room temperature. Using a coffee filter or mesh strainer, strain the syrup into an airtight container or squeeze bottle for easy use. Store in the refrigerator for up to 4 weeks.

Grenadine

Tools: saucepan, wooden spoon, airtight container or squeeze bottle

2 cups 100 percent pomegranate juice

2 cups granulated sugar

Many people mistakenly think that grenadine is a cherry-flavored syrup because it's used in cherry colas and Shirley Temples, but it's actually a sweetened pomegranate syrup. There is something special about a homemade grenadine syrup—it has more bright, tart flavors than the overly sweet, store-bought kind.

▸ In a medium saucepan, bring the pomegranate juice to a boil over medium-high heat. Add the sugar and stir until it has dissolved. Remove from the heat and let cool to room temperature. Pour the grenadine into an airtight container or squeeze bottle for easy use. Store in the refrigerator for up to 4 weeks.

Agave-Ginger Syrup

Tools: saucepan, wooden spoon, mesh strainer, airtight container or squeeze bottle

1 cup water

½ medium ginger root, sliced

1½ cups agave syrup

This ginger-infused agave syrup works wonderfully in many different cocktail recipes, especially those with ginger beer in them. Simply boiling fresh ginger with water and mixing in agave syrup creates a quick and easy cocktail syrup packed with sweet and spicy ginger flavors. Freshly sliced ginger root is the trick to this recipe—using pickled ginger, ginger powder, or candied ginger will not get the same results.

▶ In a medium saucepan, bring the water to a boil over medium-high heat. Stir in the sliced ginger, reduce the heat, and let the mixture simmer for 15 minutes. Add the agave syrup and stir until dissolved. Remove from the heat and let cool to room temperature. Using a mesh strainer to remove the ginger pieces, pour the syrup into an airtight container or squeeze bottle for easy use. Store in the refrigerator for up to 4 weeks.

Chamoy Syrup

Tools: saucepan, wooden spoon, blender, airtight container

3 dried ancho chile peppers

6 fresh apricots, pitted and chopped

1 cup dried apricots or 1 cup apricot jam

½ cup prunes, seeded

⅓ cup freshly squeezed lime juice

1 cup brown sugar

½ teaspoon salt

½ teaspoon lime zest

1 tablespoon tamarind pulp (optional)

3 cups water

Chamoy is a deep red–colored condiment from Mexico that is usually served as a dip for fresh fruit or used as a rim for nectar beverages or cocktails. It is also typically served sprinkled with chile-lime seasoning like Tajín. If you can't find chamoy syrup in your local stores, it's easy to make at home and tastes way better than the store-bought version.

▸ In a saucepan over medium-high heat, combine the chile peppers, fresh and dried apricots, prunes, lime juice, brown sugar, salt, lime zest, tamarind pulp (if using), and water and bring to a boil over medium-high heat. Reduce the heat to low and simmer for 30 minutes, until the liquid reduces by about two-thirds. Make sure to stir occasionally when the mixture starts bubbling to prevent it from burning. Remove from the heat and let cool to room temperature. Once cooled, transfer the mixture to a blender and puree until smooth. If the chamoy seems too thick, you can add a little bit of water to thin it out. Transfer to an airtight container and store in the refrigerator for up to 2 weeks.

Traditional Margarita, page 28

Measurement Conversions

VOLUME EQUIVALENTS	U.S. STANDARD	U.S. STANDARD (OUNCES)	METRIC (APPROXIMATE)
LIQUID	2 tablespoons	1 fl. oz.	30 mL
	¼ cup	2 fl. oz.	60 mL
	½ cup	4 fl. oz.	120 mL
	1 cup	8 fl. oz.	240 mL
	1½ cups	12 fl. oz.	355 mL
	2 cups or 1 pint	16 fl. oz.	475 mL
	4 cups or 1 quart	32 fl. oz.	1 L
	1 gallon	128 fl. oz.	4 L
DRY	⅛ teaspoon	—	0.5 mL
	¼ teaspoon	—	1 mL
	½ teaspoon	—	2 mL
	¾ teaspoon	—	4 mL
	1 teaspoon	—	5 mL
	1 tablespoon	—	15 mL
	¼ cup	—	59 mL
	⅓ cup	—	79 mL
	½ cup	—	118 mL
	⅔ cup	—	156 mL
	¾ cup	—	177 mL
	1 cup	—	235 mL
	2 cups or 1 pint	—	475 mL
	3 cups	—	700 mL
	4 cups or 1 quart	—	1 L
	½ gallon	—	2 L
	1 gallon	—	4 L

OVEN TEMPERATURES

FAHRENHEIT	CELSIUS (APPROXIMATE)
250°F	120°C
300°F	150°C
325°F	165°C
350°F	180°C
375°F	190°C
400°F	200°C
425°F	220°C
450°F	230°C

Resources

Bowen, Sarah. *Divided Spirits: Tequila, Mezcal, and the Politics of Production*. Berkeley, CA: University of California Press, 2015.

Craddok, Harry. *The Savoy Cocktail Book*. Mansfield Centre, CT: Martino Publishing, 2015. First published 1930.

Janzen, Emma. *Mezcal: The History, Craft & Cocktails of the World's Ultimate Artisanal Spirit*. Beverly, MA: Voyageur Press, 2017.

Salcido, Joel. *The Spirit of Tequila*. San Antonia, TX: Trinity University Press, 2017.

Taste Tequila (blog). TasteTequila.com.

Thomas, Jerry. *How to Mix Drinks, or The Bon-Vivant's Companion*. Kansas City, MO: Andrews McMeel Publishing, 2015. First published in 1862.

Index

About the Author

Restaurant consultant **Bentley Hale** brings more than 20 years of industry experience to the table. She specializes in new restaurant openings, focusing on concept development, food and beverage recipe development, and operational support. Hale has held positions in both general manager and beverage director roles with corporate and privately owned companies.

Teaching staff-training seminars, creating bar menus, and planning wine-pairing dinners throughout her career helped Hale realize her passion for wine and spirit education. Her enthusiasm for teaching others about the diverse world of wine and spirits led her to start Sip Happens Wine School, which focuses on making wine and spirit education practical and fun.

Alongside working in the restaurant industry, Hale graduated from the Art Institute in California with a bachelor of science in interior design. Her thesis focused on restaurant design and marketing. In her spare time, you can catch her frequenting new restaurants, strolling through farmers' markets, or perusing thrift shops for vintage cocktail glasses.

CPSIA information can be obtained
at www.ICGtesting.com
Printed in the USA
JSHW011201130222
22793JS00002B/2